From Question to Quest

Your Route to Transformation

KRISHNA RUPARELIA

WOW Book Publishing™

Table of Contents

From Question to Quest:
Your Route to Transformation

First Edition Published by Krishna Ruparelia

Copyright © 2021 Krishna Ruparelia

WOW Book Publishing™

ISBN: 9781686079771

All rights reserved. Neither this book nor any parts within it may be sold or reproduced in any form without permission. No part of this book may be reproduced in any form or by any electronic or mechanical means including information storage and retrieval systems, without permission in writing from the author.

The only exception is by a reviewer, who may quote short excerpts in a review. The purpose of this book is to educate and entertain. The views and opinions expressed in this book are that of the author based on her personal experiences and education. The author does not guarantee that anyone following the techniques, suggestions, ideas or strategies will become successful.

The author shall neither be liable nor responsible for any loss or damage allegedly arising from any information or suggestion in this book.

From Question to Quest

"Our deepest fear is not that we are inadequate. Our deepest fear is that we are powerful beyond measure. It is our light, not our darkness, that most frightens us.

We ask ourselves, who am I to be brilliant, gorgeous, talented, fabulous? Actually, who are you not to be? You are a child of God. Your playing small does not serve the world. There is nothing enlightened about shrinking so that other people won't feel insecure around you.

We are all meant to shine, as children do. We were born to make manifest the glory of God that is within us. It's not just in some of us; it's in everyone.

As we let our own light shine, we unconsciously give other people permission to do the same. As we are liberated from our own fear, our presence automatically liberates others."

—Nelson Mandela

Table of Contents

From Question to Quest

Table of Contents

TABLE OF CONTENTS 5
TESTIMONIALS 7
ACKNOWLEDGEMENTS 13
DEAR READER 17
AUTHOR'S PAGE 19
FOREWORD 23
WHY READ THIS BOOK? 25
ABOUT THE AUTHOR 27
CHAPTER 1 31
    THE DAY I DIED — 13TH MAY 2002 31
    THE FINAL SIX MINUTES: 36
    13TH MAY 2002 38
CHAPTER 2 51
    IN AFRICA — THE UNKNOWN QUEST BEGINS 51
    SEVA (SERVICE) DAY: 24TH MAY 2002 57
CHAPTER 3 63
    WHO AM I? 63
    LESSON 1: FORGIVE YOURSELF — 68
    LESSON 2: HOW WE EXPERIENCE THE WORLD? 69
    LESSON 3: HEARING 70
    LESSON 4: SPEECH 73
    LESSON 5: SMELL 73

~ 5 ~

Table of Contents

    Lesson 6: Sight 73
    Lesson 7: Touch 74
    The Seven Layers of Existence 76

CHAPTER 4 .... **81**
    Healing the wounded heart 81

CHAPTER 5 .... **91**
    The profundity of serving others 91

CHAPTER 6 .... **109**
    Finding the divine in Yoga 109

CHAPTER 7 .... **119**
    My life, my responsibility 119

CHAPTER 8.1 .... **133**
    A Paradigm shift 133

CHAPTER 8.2 .... **141**
    The hidden jewels 141

CHAPTER 9 .... **149**
    The love that you seek 149

CHAPTER 10 .... **159**
    The power of surrender 159

CHAPTER 11 .... **171**
    Connecting the Dots 171

RESOURCES **183**

Testimonials

Krishna is an inspiring leadership coach who loves to help others grow to who they are meant to be. She has a passion for life that's addictive and has so much wisdom to share with the world. The results she delivers to her clients are impeccable.

Sheetal Thaker
Digital Transformation Expert
And Agile Consultant

Krishna is a dedicated yoga teacher who has a deep calling to serve her community through her passion and dedication to spreading yoga as practice to promote wellness. Having seen the feedback from her yoga students during lockdown, she is helping them to remain calm when all they want to do is scream. She has passed on breathing techniques that a doctor has used to help patients deal with COVID 19 symptoms.

Umesh Solanki
Digital Manager, and Volunteer for,
The International Association for Human Values

Testimonials

Krishna is an experienced coach who knows and applies the most important tools. She is a positive, enthusiastic and energetic coach: typical of her 'yellow energy', she is enthusiastic, communicates clearly and has a natural ability to inspire confidence. She could quickly assess and support me (as a Coachee).

Rafael Nascimento
Marketing and Innovation Manager

I hired Krishna to work with my global clients to deliver a leadership programme and, as expected, she exceeded both my expectations and the clients'. Krishna is transparent, honest and prompt. You know exactly where you stand and this is incredibly refreshing. When Krishna commits to any task she commits wholeheartedly, her communication style is both encouraging and passionate. As a coach, she can take anyone on a journey.

Mamta Saha
Occupational Psychologist,
Coach, and TEDx Speaker

From Question to Quest

Krish is a highly thorough, focused and yet agile coach, she brings a wealth of experience, supported by tools and methodologies along with high energy and passion to help. I met Krish at WBS, being our careers coach while I was at crossroads and contemplating my next step(s).

In the very first meeting I could see the value she adds. She supported me very efficiently and effectively and helped me understand my professional strengths and opportunities.

She did a mock interview with me and 5 minutes in I forgot it was a mock one, the complete experience was outstanding along with getting constructive prompt and thorough feedback, which helps me even today.

She is very knowledgeable in and around her field and very personable, she does coaching in a tailored fashion to suit candidates' needs. She is a coach who delivers value!

Siddartha Jain
Product Innovation, Development and Delivery Consultant

Testimonials

Krish has a wonderful light touch and can offer calm and precise insight in her approach. She draws on broad experience and deftly selects from this to support a greater level of awareness and a better understanding of those she works with.

Desiree Ashton
Academy Lead-The Wellbeing Project

Krishna has a huge amount of energy as well as enthusiasm when she works with clients. She maintains an incredible sense of positivity and provides active coaching, drawing on her vast toolkit of coaching techniques and methodologies. I would recommend anyone looking to make a career change or seek advancement to work with Krish.

Fiona Bennett
Finance Change and Transformation Leader

These days I advise all my patients, friends and relatives to practice pranayama breathing taught by Krishna because I can feel the difference and I know it helps to increase the immunity which we all need during these uncertain times; thank you Krishna.

Dr Sashi Mehta

It was evident that Krish would become a great yoga teacher as she is very dedicated to yoga and shares the benefits with everyone she meets. Krish is very passionate about helping others and sharing her positive outlook and knowledge.

Lisa Ward
Hatha Yoga Teacher

Krish embodies such great values. She is a compassionate and caring person who reached out to me when I was looking for the next step in my career when I hit a crossroad. She supported me in enhancing the depths of my sense of my professional self.

Ali Mehdi
Consultant, and Orthopaedic Surgeon,

Testimonials

Krish has a wonderful energy and strives to make the best of her life. Having worked with Krish on a consultancy basis, it's clear she has a passion for living by her spiritual values. I found her commitment to people's wellbeing and personal development inspiring.

Cecilia Shandeva
Founder - workplace wellbeing and resilience
www.yugenconnections.com

Acknowledgements

There are so many people to thank and give gratitude for the manifestation of this book. I am indebted to the divinity and the higher power for supporting me along my life's journey.

I would like to thank the universe for bringing precious jewels of yoga and Kriya into my life. It has transformed me as I have found my passion, purpose and fulfillment.

Thank you to my inspiration H.H Sri Sri Ravi Shankar for guiding me to feel joy and gratitude! I feel free!

I would like to thank all my past teachers: Buddha, Rumi, Napoleon Hill, Gandhi, Mark Twain, Patanjali (Yoga Sutras), and Steve Jobs, who are still leaving footprints on the human mind to this day.

My teachers Vishen Lakhiani, Tony Robbins, Dr. John Gottman, Dr. John Demartini, Elizabeth Gilbert, Jack Canfield, Deepak Chopra, Jon and

Acknowledgements

Missy Butcher, Michael Fischman, Robin Sharma, Dr. Bruce Lipton, and Dr. Khalsa (Harvard Medical School) who have really helped me along my journey to live life at an extraordinary level. Thank you to Vishal Morjaria and the team at WOW Book Camp for believing in my dream of becoming an Author.

Thank you to the Art of Living Foundation (www.artofliving.org/uk-en) for their spiritual contribution in uplifting humanity and bringing joy and peace to millions of people worldwide.

Thank you to the Tumaini Children's Home of Hope in Mombasa for the beautiful work they are doing. Helping and supporting orphaned and vulnerable children infected and affected by HIV and Aids.

I acknowledge my parents — my father, no longer in this physical realm, who taught me many valuable lessons that shine through my life today.

To my mother who is my rock "Thank you, Mum. Thank you for believing in my dreams." Thank you to my family. Each one of you have played a pivotal role in shaping who I am today.

From Question to Quest

Thank you to my beautiful fur-baby, Milo, who is a bundle of unconditional love. I am blessed to have a kind soul to share my love with. He has taught me play, presence and being grateful for the smallest of things. To my friend, Dr. Gurpreet Singh, for believing in my dreams and walking with me along this journey as an aspiring Author. Your friendship is a true blessing.

Thank you to the Wow Book Camp Team— Vishal Morjaria for Wow Book Camp training, Pauline Barath for being so patient and holding my hand through the publishing process. Thank you immensely to the editing team.

Most importantly, I want to thank you for taking the time to join me on this quest. I want you to feel inspired in achieving your dreams and know that you are not here to play small. That a life of growing, giving and contribution is all that matters.

With love, light and gratitude. Namaste!

Krish xxx

Acknowledgements

From Question to Quest

Dear Reader

The information within this book, including the opinions expressed, is based on the author's personal experience and is not intended to provide professional advice. The characters depicted in this story are fictional. Where research has been cited, you will find the references and follow-up reading at the back of the book.

The author and the publishers make no guarantees, either expressed or implied, concerning the accuracy, applicability, effectiveness, reliability, or suitability of the content. If you wish to follow the advice or recommendations mentioned in the book you take full responsibility for your actions.

The author and publisher of this book will, under no circumstances, be held liable for any direct or indirect incidental damage arising from the use of any of the information contained in this book. All content is for information only and is not guaranteed for content accuracy or any other implied or explicit purpose.

Dear Reader

From Question to Quest

Author's page

This book is a work of fiction. It's a story about Maaya Thacker, a girl in her thirties. Broken and grief stricken after her Fathers' death, combined with her marital separation, grief stricken and feeling a deep void in life Maaya embarks on a quest to search for answers. Trying to make sense of her pain she travels to Africa and begins to awaken to what truly matters in life.

She learns that she was meant to be on the Earth for a bigger purpose and surrenders to a grander plan.

Gandhi says that; "The greatest way to find yourself is losing yourself in the service of others," and that is what she does. In volunteering for the needy, she finds the most precious treasure ever and she heals through giving.

In giving, she receives the unimaginable. A treasure that she never knew existed. The treasure of connecting with the human spirit. She finds herself and life is changed forever. The lessons that

Author's page

Maaya learns through this extraordinary adventure will create wonderful changes in your life as well. How do I know this? Because, they are the lessons that have transformed mine. I suffered from anxiety while at university, struggling at school, often failing at exams. My anxiety increased and my performance in my studies suffered. For years I hung on to the story that I wasn't good at anything.

My worries about succeeding in exams increased, combined with such low esteem. It was then that someone randomly suggested a weekly yoga class which I ended up attending for a number of years. Little did I know that yoga would really be the practise that would change my life. Following the completion of my studies, my father suddenly passed away.

Grief-stricken and feeling a deep void in life, I began searching for answers. This was the beginning of my spiritual inquisition. As the years went by, I would often find myself feeling empty, numb and incomplete with my own existence despite flourishing in my career and pursuing my goals.

From Question to Quest

My search for something deeper still prevailed. Fear and anguish combined with the hollow emptiness continued to amplify as I found myself oscillating between the highs and lows of life's rollercoaster.

At age 34, I discovered the 'Art of Living Happiness' course and my life transformed. Practising the Sudarshan Kriya technique has transformed me in gaining so much more of a balance in my emotions and my life. Less stress, greater resilience, clarity in my thinking, awareness in my soul and life has become a pilgrimage of growth and adventure. It is enriching to be on this journey.

Life is no less than a celebration. Nowadays, yoga and Kriya have become such an integrated way of life, such that I was deeply compelled to write this book to share my learnings with the intention that you will benefit from these profound techniques and wisdom. I am always a beginner in this journey of personal growth and the spirit of enquiry unfolds at every step I take.

I sincerely hope that 'Question to Quest' propels you to take the leap of your personal journey into

Author's page

life's deeper question of who you are, so you can unravel and dive deep into life's sacred treasures. I encourage you to learn the pearls of wisdom in this book which will inspire you to become resourceful and create meaning in setbacks and trials so that you can live a life of meaning, purpose and fulfilment. If you really want to apply the learnings, please share what knowledge and enlightenment you gain with someone within 24 hours of completing the book. This will consolidate your own learning and help you integrate the wisdom into your own life.

I also hope that you adopt a sense of wonderment and curiosity while reading this memoir. Go beyond and believe in the miraculous, for this is the beautiful blessing that life bestows on us. I hope that you will spread the learnings and touch the lives of others. I know you will make a difference. Travel light, be the light, share the light.

With my deepest gratitude...

Krish xx

Foreword

Dear Reader,

'Question to Quest' is the book you need to read in order to tap into your personal power. The knowledge in this book has the power to help you create the life that you truly deserve and desire. This book shares practical wisdom on how to create meaning from the events that occur in your life, rekindling your faith to transform yourself.

Krishna is an inspiring HR professional, with 15 years' experience and has a passion for self-transformation and growth and authentically shows up in her life to create her best self. Her expertise is a testimonial to her mission in enabling others to live a life of purpose, passion and impact.

Vishal Morjaria
Award-Winning Author
and International Speaker

Foreword

From Question to Quest

Why read this book?

Seven billion people live on a planet which circles a ball of fire next to a moon that moves the sea. This is a miracle. The universe has existed for 14 billion years and will continue to do so for aeons. Moreover, astronomers believe there are around 200 billion galaxies in this universe.

We are a mere speck of dust on this macrocosm in this vast existence. The river of life can engulf us into a sea of troubled waters, where we are tossed around, riding the waves of pleasure and pain.

How do we create meaning in our lives in a frantic world, when everything is changing? Between the gushing waters of pleasure and pain, flows the river of life. If we spend too much time on one side—we will miss out on the jewels of moments that make up our life.

Yet within us, there is a deep longing to know our true selves. Come on this adventure with me and dare to ask yourself some of the deepest questions that have puzzled mankind since the beginning of time.

Why read this book?

- Can we transform our pain into power and create peace within ourselves?
- Is passion, purpose and fulfilment a possibility?
- Can you go deep inside yourself and ask the question; "Who am I?"

Maaya's journey is about one woman's quest in searching for herself and unleashing her own power to manifest a life of meaning and celebration!

'Question to Quest' will teach you:

- Powerful ways to conquer stress, develop resilience, transform negative emotions into love and compassion and make life a celebration.
- How to listen to the whispers of your heart to find your passion and purpose.
- How to ignite adventure, simplicity, and curiosity into your life.
- Practical wisdom to help cultivate your best life.

From Question to Quest

About the Author

Krishna qualified in BSC (Hons) in Psychology and Management from Aston Business School, in Birmingham, UK. Since then she has successfully worked for a number of blue-chip organization's and specializes in leadership development, transformation, and change.

Krishna's mission is to empower others to unleash their own potential, help people find their passion, purpose, and live a life of abundance and fulfilment. In her spare time, Krishna teaches Hatha yoga and loves to travel, write and cook delicious cuisine.

Learn more about Krishna at:

www.unshakableresilience.com

Download links, a reading group guide and other features are available at:

www.unshakableresilience.com

About the Author

From Question to Quest

Dear Babaji,

You have GONE and I am still searching for YOU.

WHERE ARE YOU?

<SILENCE>

About the Author

From Question to Quest

Chapter 1

The day I died – 13th May 2002

"The wound is the place where light enters you"
— Rumi

My name is Maaya Roshni Thacker. I am 33 years old. I live in a small town named Bolton in the northwest of England. I was born in Northwick Park Hospital in North London on the 13th of Feb 1986. My parents migrated to the UK 30 years after the Idi Amin saga that expelled thousands of Asians to leave Africa.

Life is drifting along...nothing exciting, quite mundane to be honest. Mediocre; I am plodding along. In less than 24 hours, I WILL BE DEAD. Yes, you heard me. DEAD. My whole entire existence as Maaya Roshni Thacker, destroyed in an instant.

There will be NOTHING!

NO TRACE OF MY EXISTENCE WILL REMAIN.

Chapter 1

At 7.30 am, my father, Babaji, called my name. "Maaya—are you there?" he said as I ran upstairs.

"What's the matter Baba?" I asked.

"I have a headache." He replied. Babaji was struggling along the upstairs passage to reach the bathroom, kneeling against the wall. Maa had gone out to the Hare Krishna Mandir temple in Watford. "Hold on Babaji!" I yelled, running downstairs to get some orange juice. Baba was diabetic and I thought that his blood sugar level might have dropped.

"Drink this, Baba." I said, quickly running back to his bedroom. A few minutes later Baba knelt against his bed looking pale and weak. I decided to call my older brother, Govind, who lived 10 minutes away. "Baba is not well. Can you pop round? He is not responding, and his speech is slurring. He is complaining of a headache." I said nervously.

Govind quickly rushed over and gave Baba a slice of banana, but within minutes Baba vigorously vomited.

At that moment we called an ambulance.

From Question to Quest

8 minutes later...

8.15am

The ambulance arrived.

Adrian, the paramedic was very calm and checked Baba's pulse.

"He isn't responding." Govind said.

I didn't really understand what they were doing. He looked so pale. Head turned to one side, wearing only a vest and an off-white cotton kurta pyjama (linen trousers), as the paramedics placed him in a wheelchair and rolled him into the ambulance.

8.45am

30 minutes passed by and checks were being done. I went outside, knocked on the ambulance door, but there was no answer. I went back inside the house and stared outside the living room front window, puzzled to see what was going on. Just then, Adrian rang the doorbell.

Chapter 1

"We will need to rush him to A&E. Your father has had a stroke." he said.

Govind went in the ambulance with Baba. Before I knew it, the ambulance swiftly drove off heading to the Royal Bolton Hospital. I stayed behind and called Maa, telling her to hurry home.

11.30am

Maa and I arrived at the hospital. We approached the Sandringham building and rushed towards ward 22.

"We are looking for Ramesh Mathur Thacker?" I asked one of the nurses, who directed us to the room. I opened the door and stood frozen in disbelief. Babaji was breathing heavily, strapped to an oxygen mask, unconscious and unaware of what was going on around him. Maa broke down when I hugged her.

"I can't believe it. I shouldn't have left him and gone to the mandir, I should have stayed at home." Maa said with tears rolling down her cheeks.

From Question to Quest

I felt really scared. Maa and I clung to each other, frightened of what was ahead of us. A few minutes later, a barrage of doctors and nurses came into the room with the lead consultant, Dr. Sharma, who spoke to Govind.

"Your father has had a massive stroke. It doesn't look very good I'm afraid." the doctor said.

The next eight hours were a blur. Things happened so fast it was hard to digest what was going on. Relatives suddenly arrived from London and Manchester. One of Maa's friends, Laxmi Mosi (Aunty), came over and bought some Jal (holy water) from the mandir. Maa poured a few drops of Jal onto Baba's lips. Baba's sister, Jyothi Aunty, a Sai Baba Devotee brought some Vibhuti (sacred ash).

Maa took some blessed Vibhuti and sprinkled it on Baba's forehead, as it was considered sacred and holy. At 1.22 am, fifteen close friends and relatives, Chaacha (Uncle), Chaachi (Aunty), all congregated around Baba's hospital bed, witnessing this very moment. Baba's breath was fading away.

Chapter 1

A pretty, young nurse came over to check up on him. As she checked the oxygen levels she quietly said, "We are just making him comfortable."

THE FINAL SIX MINUTES:

We all prayed OM NAMAH SHIVAYA, OM NAMAH SHIVAYA reciting these prayers loudly in quiet desperation. Maa clenched my hand tightly while wiping away her floods of tears.

The emotions in the room were intense; Baba was disappearing. He was coming to an end. We had no control. He was slipping away. There was nothing we could do.

At 1.29 am he vomited a trickle of blood, exhaled his last breath, and left the world.

FINISHED…

GONE…

EXTINGUISHED…

DECEASED…

From Question to Quest

GONE...

GONE...

GONE...

That was the moment I DIED...

I froze motionless. Pain flooded my veins like venom. My chest tightened and I struggled to breathe, gasping for air. My heartbeat was racing. The saliva in my mouth dried up. I was engulfed in a storm of grief. I cried so uncontrollably, weeping, like an abandoned child. Emptiness moved through my body like a serpent, slithering erratically, swirling from the pit of my stomach to the depth of my soul. I made my way home with my family.

As we walked along the hospital corridor, the smoky, grey sky directed us through the tunnel of darkness we found ourselves in. I noticed the full moon casting a beam of light directing us towards the car.

. . . And we went home, WITHOUT BABA.

Chapter 1

In the Hindu tradition, when someone dies, we have a 14-day mourning period ritual, where people come and sit and sing bhajans (devotional songs) to provide some comfort as a sign of respect. It is believed that the soul gains peace through the prayers and the bhajans for their onward journey.

13th May 2002

The next morning, Govind came home, sobbing relentlessly.

"I can't believe it. Baba has gone. How are we going to cope?" He said, distraught.

Maa tried to console him. We all started to prepare for the sabha (congregation). People were informed. Funeral arrangements were being made. My phone was continuously ringing with relatives conveying their condolences.

An avalanche of emotions erupted through my abdomen, shooting a dagger into my chest. Life felt like a swirling black hole and I was uncontrollably evaporating into this vortex with nowhere to turn.

From Question to Quest

The pain was an ugly reflection of me that I could not recognize.

Govind and my two cousins left to drive to Birtwhistle's Funeral Parlour to bathe the body, as part of a Hindu ritual. My brothers and cousins were guided by the priest at the funeral parlour while repeating the mantra Om Shanti Om (I am peace). Baba's body was cleansed with a mixture of milk, yogurt, ghee (clarified butter), honey and purified water.

My sister, Gita, and I arrived at the funeral parlour to pay our final respects after the dressing ritual was completed. I felt petrified and could feel a numbness circulating through my body. As we entered the room my knees trembled and my palms were sweaty.

The Om Namah Shivaya mantra was humming in the background. As I slowly opened the door to the room, there he lay, my father. Enveloped in peace. He was smiling…no longer suffering. I stood there like a statue, staring at his vibrant face with a red tikka (powder made of vermillion paste) on his forehead. He was dressed in a navy-blue pinstripe suit and seemed profoundly at peace.

Chapter 1

I touched his face. I knelt, bursting into floods of tears, bowing to him. Maa told me that I should seek forgiveness for any wrongdoings so I stayed kneeling and pleaded to him to forgive me for every time I had disappointed him and for my shortcomings. With tears streaming down my face, the pain rose again to the surface. My whole life was shattered.

As I closed my eyes, I held onto the mantra, wishing it would quench my pain. I wished the earth's crust would open up so that I could merge into it.

Afterwards, we got in the car and returned home just as relatives started to arrive from all over the world. So much was happening at home. Food was being prepared and funeral arrangements were being organised. Govind announced that the funeral would be held on the 17th of May.

On the day of the funeral, I noticed the outer world on Revenue Street remained exactly the same. People walking, travelling to work, cars passing by like normal. In contrast my world was drastically different. I was completely broken. I thought that things would never be the same again and broke down, dazzled in disbelief. It was the permanency of not knowing where people go that tormented my mind.

Pain arrived intermittently like an unwanted guest, invading my body as I danced to its tune.

Just then, Govind called, "Maaya, we need you!"

I obediently ran downstairs. All siblings co-operated, like never before, without any arguments. There was an awkward silence among us as we avoided eye contact.

The echoes of silence felt like a sharp blade cutting through air as we swam in our own anguish.

"The body will arrive at our home at 11.30 am." Govind said in a straight-faced monotone manner.

"The priest will perform the rituals and all immediate family members will say a prayer and take part in a puja (prayer ritual). Thereafter, we will go to the Gilroes Cemetery for the cremation where I will say a speech, followed by Prasad (blessed food) served at home for all the relatives that attend the funeral."

Chapter 1

As the body arrived, many people congregated around the coffin. The priest recited verses in Sanskrit. So many people, one by one, with flower petals in their hands circled the casket to pay their respects and convey their presence. As I stood frozen during the puja, I couldn't help but notice an elderly man on crutches, limping, attempting to walk around the coffin.

Baba's words echoed in my ear, "Who will cry when you die? Live in a world where, when you are gone, you are smiling but others are crying for the legacy you have left behind. This is the true essence of life." I recalled those words so vividly.

At 12.15pm, we arrived at the cemetery, accompanied by my siblings. The funeral car waited for us. Revenue Street—half blocked off. The whole journey to the cemetery was a blur. As we entered the crematorium hall, the mantra OM was playing in the background. Floral arrangements read, 'We love you Baba'. Another tribute read— 'Our beloved Dada' (Grandpa). This was fondly dedicated by my Nephew and Niece, Aaran and Anoushka. One hundred and fifty people stood in silence.

From Question to Quest

Govind gave a heart wrenching speech, mainly reminiscing about Baba's character, his drive for never giving up despite the trials of his life; from the time he came from East Africa, losing his very successful business, to the time where his health started to deteriorate. I saw strangers, acquaintances and familiar faces. I saw relatives, and neighbours that had all come to pay their respects. However, someone was missing. Raj was nowhere to be seen.

Raj was my husband. We had been married for five years, and I had met him when I was at college. We were separated at the moment. I would have thought he would have had the courtesy to phone and send his condolences. But there was no sign of him. After the funeral was over we returned home and served prasad (blessed food) as part of another ritual. The more people that ate after the funeral, the greater the blessings Baba would reap for his soul's onward journey.

As the funeral rituals came to a close, people left one by one and, by 7pm, the house was empty. Only Maa and I remained. Our home was an eerie space with just Maa and me.

Chapter 1

The silence echoed discreetly. I heard the clock ticking. Tik Tok. Tik Tok. I looked at Maa. We had nothing to say. I sat on the burgundy sofa in the lounge and noticed a picture of Babaji mounted on the wooden cabinet, with a fresh red and white garland of roses, hanging on the picture frame. A tea light candle was lit in front of the photo. Maa was washing the dishes and I was staring blankly into space in a daze, as I was consumed by the sudden emptiness that occupied the space.

On the 19th of May, it was time to return to work, and yet I was far from ready. As I applied my makeup, I knew that this was going to be my mask to disguise the melancholy I was feeling.

Attempting to camouflage my pain, I coated my pale skin with another layer of foundation. My boss, Karen Bailey, invited me into her office. I burst into tears. I tried to hold back but cried uncontrollably. My mascara ran down my cheeks and smudged my foundation.

I looked like a mess. "Maaya, I am very, very sorry for your loss." She said.

From Question to Quest

After a few minutes of trying to compose myself, I asked her how things were in the team and what updates I had to catch up on.

"We are going through really difficult times in the business..." There was a long pause from her then she continued.

"I am sorry, but we will be closing this office down. We are sorry to say your job will cease to exist." She said.

I sat there in disbelief. I was completely shocked and shaken-up.

"We will pay you your redundancy money but you will be leaving this Friday. You will be on garden leave for the next 4 weeks. If you want to go home and reflect, please take the rest of the day off. I know this is the worst possible time right now. Unfortunately, the business isn't doing well." Karen said, handing me a letter.

The whole day was bleak. I felt empty. I didn't know how to get from one moment to the next. I felt like my whole life was tossed into thin air like a pancake. I felt out of control, twisted and turned upside down. I just about got home in one piece,

Chapter 1

and I walked into an empty house. Maa was at work. I could hear the clock ticking. The plate of Prasad (blessed food) was left at the centre of the table, untouched. It seemed Maa had performed the Aarti (Hindu religious ritual of worship) today. Just then, the phone rang.

"Maaya, how was your day?" Govind asked.

"It was okay. How was yours?" I asked.

"Fine." He replied... then silence in the conversation.

"Maaya, Baba has left you an envelope. I am going to come round with it in ten minutes." Govind said and he hung up.

Maa arrived home at this point.

"Maa, Govind is coming over. He wants to give me an envelope that Baba left." I said, shrugging my shoulders.

Maa's eyes gazed at the floor. "Do you know what is in the letter?" I asked.

From Question to Quest

"I do, but your Baba had written it for you six months ago. He said he had to share something with you." She replied.

When my brother arrived he looked emotionally drained, with dark circles under his eyes and a subdued look on his face. Govind pulled out the letter from his coat pocket and looked at Maa. Maa came closer to sit next to me.

"This is for you Maaya. Why don't you go to your room and read this in your own time." She said, in a quiet voice.

"What's in it?" I questioned.

"Come on just tell me. What's in it?"

Before Maa could reply, I rushed to my bedroom alone, sat down and closed the door. I opened the letter.

This is what I read: 'Maaya Beti (beloved daughter), by the time you read this letter I will not be here. I know you are feeling very much troubled with what has happened with Raj. I want you to fulfil my wish. I want you to go to Africa, my birth place, and I want you to give something back. I

Chapter 1

have faith in you that you can do this Maaya. Love, Baba.'

I re-read the letter twice. My eyeballs popping out, bewildered at this request. How was I going to step out alone, when I could barely remember my own name, let alone go to AFRICA? I quickly ran downstairs.

"Maa, Baba wants me to go to Africa. He wants me to go and do what he could not. I am clueless Maa." I said. "They are relocating the offices of Bluebell. They said they will be making people redundant. What am I going to do Maa?" I said panicking.

"Calm down." Maa said, as I started to blubber.

"Maybe it's a sign Maaya." She added.

"What sign?" I interrupted.

"I don't believe in stupid signs. All I know is that I am not happy. I don't want to be here anymore."

"I wish I was DEAD." I muttered.

"Maaya STOP talking like this!" Maa yelled.

From Question to Quest

"It's true, I don't WANT TO BE HERE!" I said, raising my voice, desperately wanting to be heard. I threw one of the deities from the mandir onto the floor.

"MAAYA!" Maa screamed.

"I have had enough of everything! I have had enough of this life. I want to end it right now." I wept uncontrollably.

"I am sick of my life. There is nothing here. I wish I was DEAD!" I shouted.

"You don't like anything. You run from one place to another trying to escape your misery. Tell me, where has that got you? Every time the going gets tough you want to run away. You did this growing up and you are doing it now!" Maa yelled.

I sat there sobbing, on the floor hugging my knees to my chest with my arms covering my face. A few moments passed by and then I said in a croaky voice...

"I am scared Maa, I am petrified. I don't know where my life is heading. I don't know what to do... I don't know anything anymore."

Chapter 1

"Look at me Maaya—look at me." She said."Go to Africa. Go and fulfil your Baba's dreams. He was longing to go back to Africa for many years and spoke solemnly about the life he lost there."

From Question to Quest

Chapter 2

In Africa — The unknown quest begins

*"When you cease to make a contribution,
you begin to die."*
— *Eleanor Roosevelt*

I was seated on the National Express coach heading to Heathrow Airport to fly to Mombasa. A mixture of emotions churned inside my stomach. I felt guilty for leaving Maa, so quickly after Baba's passing. Maa stood outside St Victoria bus station with tears running down her cheeks as she waved at me, her face looking glum. I listened to the Gayatri Mantra.

"This is IT! No turning back," I said, trying to convince myself.

Just then, Govind parked up by the bus station and ran towards me. I quickly got off the coach for

Chapter 2

a moment as he handed me a parcel, gift wrapped in rustic brown paper.

"Baba left this for you. You must follow the instructions in this box without fail Maaya. Do you hear me?" Govind said firmly as he hugged me tightly and nudged me to get back on the bus.

"And don't worry about Maa! I will look after her." he added waving goodbye.

I was bemused, I had no idea what was in the parcel. First; the letter and now this… My hands were shaking, my breath quivering. I sat back on my seat, and, with my knees shaking, apprehensively opened the box. I saw a bundle of letters written on bamboo leaves. Each scroll was tied with a ribbon and labelled in beautiful calligraphy.

Scroll 1 read: 'Open this as you start your journey to Africa.' I gently untied the ribbon, opening the scroll to read Baba's words, 'Focus on the inner dialogue between you and God and watch the universe unfold.'

I didn't understand what Baba meant. I mean my faith was anything but stable. In fact, I didn't even

From Question to Quest

understand the concept of God let alone have a relationship with him. I was brought up as a Hindu, Maa used to entertain me and my siblings by telling us mythical stories from the Bhagavad Gita and Ramayana.

As the years passed by, I found myself questioning the subject of religion, but had no idea how to approach the subject with Maa. She was a devout Hindu, blinded to her faith and her countless rituals. Maa simply embraced the rituals and traditions without question.

God remained an alien concept to me. I mean, was He this man in the sky who just dictated what went on in our lives? Were we just mere puppets on a stage or did we have some control? I pondered the concept all the way to the airport and through check-in.

I boarded the plane, lost in thought, and hardly noticed when the plane took off. Despite my questions about faith, I closed my eyes and attempted to pray in desperation. I covered my eyes with my palms and pleaded like a pauper.

Chapter 2

"Dear God, if you exist, I need some help right now."

I held Baba's scroll, tightly squeezing it towards my chest, desperately wishing I could get a feel of him. 'If only I could see you one more time to say a proper goodbye.' I thought, with tears streaming down my face.

After a long flight, and a four hour delay in Nairobi, my lower back felt like it had shrivelled up; the pain was agonizing and I could barely move, but finally I arrived in Mombasa. I felt exhausted from the jetlag, having not slept a wink on the plane.

The next day, as I was being taken to the children's orphanage, I noticed the chaos around Mombasa.

The disorderly traffic, the beggars on the street, the many Matatus (public mode of transport) that carried passengers, squashed together like sardines. As the Matatu stopped on the road, I noticed a beggar with five deformities all over his body struggling to move, begging for money.

From Question to Quest

Next to his donation box read a quote, 'Allah is great.' I smirked ironically. Life made no sense to me! I arrived at the Tumaini Home of Hope Children's home, founded by a British lady 25 years ago, Gill Smith. The home provided care for children affected by HIV and AIDS. Gill shared her story with me of how she was inspired after she had found a girl abandoned and left on a roundabout to die.

"I then realized that we needed to set something up here." She said. "With our help, some financial support, and volunteers we will be able to provide a better life for these innocent children." She added humbly.

I met a group of kids of different ages, from 6 months to 15 years-old, each with their own traumatic past. I met Kimji, a 7 year old chubby looking boy that had the cutest round face and a podgy belly. His mother had sadly passed away when he was born, so his Aunty had raised him.

Except she used to abuse him with cigarettes as a way of scolding him, until one day he was so petrified he ran away and Gill found him on the

Chapter 2

streets sick with fever. I noticed the faint scars on his arms as he came towards me.

"Gill," I said.

"I have come to give something back and wondered what sort of things I can do whilst I am here. My family have sent a £500 donation. What can I do to support Tumaini?" I asked.

"Well you can always give me the money and I can find a useful way of using the funds." She replied.

I shrugged my shoulders and replied politely, "That is one way, but I am here. I want to do something hands on. I have come specifically to fulfil my father's wishes, as he recently passed away. How about cooking some food for the kids? What do the kids normally eat?"

"Sukuma (Kale) & Ugali, (maize flour)." Gill replied.

"What are their favourite dishes?" I asked curiously.

From Question to Quest

"Well they love sausages, chips and ice cream." Gill replied.

"It's a luxury for them to get this food. Nakumat, our main supermarket is ten minutes from here. If you can pay for a driver, then we can ask Roy to take you there." Gill said.

"I will introduce you to Amondi, our chef who is in charge of the kitchen so you can buy all the ingredients. You can assist Amondi in the kitchen and serve the kids too." Gill said.

Seva (service) Day: 24th May 2002

As I was leaving to go back to the hostel Sukvinder, a Sikh gentleman, came into Gill's office and excitedly said, "Guruji (by the name of Sri Sri Ravi Shankar) is here if you want to visit him and take his blessings Maaya."

Gill passionately insisted "Yes, it'll be a privilege to meet this wise man. Come on, I will take you in my car." she insisted.

Chapter 2

Gill took hold of my hand and jostled me into her car. We drove towards Agha Khan Road and arrived at the Shreenathji Mandir (temple). Crowds of people had gathered around the entrance as they tried to get a glimpse of Guruji. With no space to move amongst the crowd Gill took me around the back of the entrance to avoid the chaos.

"Here you go." Gill said, giving me a bunch of tulips.

"Give this to Guruji."Gill said as I opened the door, Guruji's eyes instantly connected with mine.

Tears started to flow down my cheeks and I didn't even know why. Guruji was about 5 feet 3 inches tall with ebony-black wavy hair and beautiful almond eyes, which glowed like a laser beam. He was wearing a white cotton loincloth with a tikka on his forehead.

Born on the 13th May, 1956 in Papanasam, Tamil Nadu; Guruji was reciting the Bhagavat Gita at the age of 4 years old. At age, 6 he was often found sitting in deep meditation.

He began his interest in the Vedas and was taught by a number of prominent teachers. In 1973, he completed a degree in physics after spending time with Maharishi Mehesh yogi. In 1982, Guruji went into a 10 day silence in Shimoga and the Sudarshan kriya was born.

He looked at me.

"Betho." (sit down) He said in Hindi.

I sat down in the corner and handed him the flowers.

"Where have you come from?" He asked me in English.

"England," I replied.

"My father requested I do some seva (service) in Africa. He suddenly passed away, so I have come to fulfil his wishes."

I stared at the floor trying to disguise my gnawing pain, and then he asked.

"What is the matter, Maaya?"

I stared at him in silence for a moment and then plucked up the courage to share my woes.

"Guruji…" Tears welled up in my eyes,

Chapter 2

"I feel so broken. I have no idea which way to turn." I said, staring at the floor.

"Pain is haunting me like a ghost. I don't even know where I belong." I said.

He sat there in silence, listening attentively as he saw my eyes watering and my face swimming in sorrow.

"Anicca." He said.

"Anicca . . . Anicca." He softly muttered.

"What do you mean?" I asked.

"Everything is changing." He replied.

I smirked at him, silently mumbling to myself, "My whole life has been turned upside down. I have been catapulted into a sea of my own emotional upheaval and all he can tell me is everything is changing. I mean, seriously didn't I know that already?"

Guruji sat in silence pausing and said, "You do one thing. There is a three day happiness course I am teaching. Come. You have come here for a reason. You have many questions that are arising in your mind, is that right? Tell me when does your seva (voluntary work) start in the morning?"

"Tomorrow, at 8.30am." Gill interjected.

"Okay, well then I suggest you get up at 6.30 am, attend the programme, then go for your seva." Guruji said casually.

"6.30 am?" I asked.

"Yes." He said confidently.

"Erm…okay." I replied, looking at Gill.

"That is final then."Gill said.

Gill drove me back to my hostel. As I sat in the lobby, I was a little perplexed by the conversation with Guruji. I had no idea what I had got myself into. Out of respect I didn't want to say no but I couldn't help be a little dubious. So here I was, half-committed to begin this journey with this small, bearded man who resembled Jesus.

Cynical in my thinking, I didn't even have a clue as to what he was going to teach me, and the more I thought about it the more I resisted the moment.

Chapter 2

Then I re-read Baba's letter, which reminded me to let my journey in Africa unfold as it was meant to.

Chapter 3

Who Am I?

An unexamined life is not worth living"
—Deepak Chopra

The next day I arrived at the Mandir. Guruji was sitting in silence in a lotus position, looking serene with his eyes closed, meditating. A group of people were all sitting quietly. I could smell the pleasant burning of orange blossom and sandalwood incense.

Guruji opened his eyes and warmly welcomed us all.

"Namaste." He said, making eye contact with every person, with such presence and eloquence.

"Before we can start any new learning's, we must feel at home in our environment. I would like you all to go around, greeting everyone in the room by saying, 'I belong to you'. I want you all to greet

Chapter 3

everyone with an open heart. Introduce yourself and hug one another." He said.

At the moment of hugging and greeting each other, a cloud of shyness came over me, making my palms feel sweaty. I was really reluctant to go around hugging everyone.

As it happened, as I was introducing myself, one of the participants, Naomi, gave me the biggest hug and said, "I belong to you Maaya."

She had a beaming smile and seemed so open. How I longed for this I wondered. I could not help but reciprocate. I hugged her back and said "I belong to you", except, when I hugged her, she squeezed me so tight, lifting me off the floor and squeezing my tummy I could barely get my words out.

I could not help but break into a grin. After greeting the other people in the room, who I now knew to be Kilna, Jenny, and Brendan, I sat down feeling quite relaxed, and thought perhaps it wasn't so daunting after all.

As we sat down, Guruji explained.

From Question to Quest

"I belong to you is very powerful because it empowers us to feel comfortable in who we are and our environment. Feeling at home means feeling comfortable. Now we all belong to each other, be real and be honest and know that you are free to be yourselves. Be natural. Say what you are feeling. Don't worry about the normal fears and apprehensions. This is your home." He explained.

"LET US BEGIN." He added.

"In order to get the best out of this programme, there are some rules you will all need to follow. This life is a very precious gift. We have a responsibility to treat it with care. For the next few days, it is good to eat moderately, and stick to a vegetarian diet." At this point Guruji's assistant, Paddy, came around, serving water with lemon slices.

"Limbu pani (water) alkalizes the body's internal environment. It's a refreshing cleanser, especially in the morning, dissolving toxins from the digestive system rehydrating the body. Let's find a partner to share your life story with, and then after 10 minutes I want you to move to the next partner and listen to their story without any

Chapter 3

interruptions. Simply listen, paying 100 percent attention." Guruji said.

Here are their stories:

Brendan; a 40-year-old American entrepreneur who filed for bankruptcy, turned to alcohol, and came to Mombasa to find some solace in his own existence.

Naomi; a 30-year-old Italian girl from Florence with sparkly emerald-green eyes, and mahogany coloured wavy hair, was a former property lawyer who rejected the rat race and was determined to find her 'dharma' (purpose). Naomi had a love for animals and talked so passionately about the love of her life, her golden Labrador, Romeo, and her transition from being a meat lover to going vegan.

Kilna; a 52-year-old Canadian woman from Nova Scotia healed herself from cancer and spent her time teaching Hatha yoga.

She reminded me of Maa—sophisticated, stylish and yet humble.

Jenny; a Project Manager from Argentina, suffered from depression due to work related stress and was searching for a better way of handling life's trials and tribulations.

Then there was me, trying to understand my world, too burdened by my own baggage and the feeling of empty and pointless existence.

"There are two forces that govern our entire lives. What are they?" Guruji said, looking at Brendan for an answer.

"Pain (sukh) and pleasure (dukkha)." Guruji nodded in agreement.

"People oscillate between avoiding pain and chasing pleasure. If you look at every one of us, our motivation propels us to move towards some sort of happiness and avoid pain. Each one of you is here because you want to free yourself from some sort of pain, the pain that cages you. Before we can move on from our story, we need to let go of the past." Guruji said.

Chapter 3

Lesson 1: Forgive yourself —

RIGHT THIS MOMENT

<Pause>

"Forgiving, means letting go of the past and remembering that you did your best at any given moment. You behaved in a certain way. You acted and things happened." Guruji said

The room was silent as everyone listened attentively.

"Maaya let go!" Guruji said firmly, looking directly into my eyes.

I stared at him. I wondered if he knew what I was experiencing.

"Forgive yourself; right now! Right this moment." He emphasized, still looking directly into my eyes.

From Question to Quest

Lesson 2: How we experience the world?

"Let us look at the six senses that enable us to experience our world. The body experiences the world through these senses. The first sense is taste. Close your eyes." Guruji said.

"Take your hand in front of your mouth and imagine that you are holding a lemon. Firstly, visualise the lemon in your hand. Now visualize biting into it. As you bite into this lemon feel the juice swirling around your mouth. Now, taste the refreshing taste of this lemon. Stay with the oozing sensations at every moment." Guruji said.

A few minutes passed by then Guruji said, "Now open your eyes."

"What happened?" Asked Guruji.

"My mouth started to salivate Guruji." Kilna replied.

Guruji nodded, "Yes! See, logically we know that there was no lemon in your hand, however the brain and body came into action as soon as you instructed your brain and visualized a lemon." He explained.

Chapter 3

"This is a habit. You all have come to know the taste of lemon." He added.

"Now suppose you like the taste of gulabjaman (sweet fried milk balls). Tell me, how much can you eat? After eating too much, it will make you ill. Too much focus on satisfying this need and what do you see? Obsession of satisfying this sensation…

Excessive indulgence to gratification will only disrupt the body's harmony and pollute the mind. In today's society we have a problem with obesity. There is no control over how much people are eating".

Lesson 3: Hearing

"As you hear something; whatever it may be. You are filtering out information, assessing, making your own evaluations and making an overall assessment. So what kind of judgments and assumptions are you making at this very moment? Are you making those judgements that serve your existence or destroy your self-worth?" Guruji asked.

"Something to think about..." He said, provoking our thinking.

"Have you noticed that Europe has over 70 percent rates of depression right now? People are complaining about this and complaining about that. Listening to the negativity around you results in the depletion of your energy. When you share your complaints, your energy diminishes. You feel exhausted. Still you keep chewing on your woes. Like chewing gum."

"How do you become more conscious Guruji?" Kilna asked.

"Sometimes we are not in control of who we interact with or the situation we find ourselves in." She said naively.

"First start to notice your energy levels. What energy are we bringing to others around us? How positive is our vibration? The very first step in any situation is awareness. Simply noticing…Then you must decide how you are going to leave people in a

Chapter 3

better state of mind than how they are at the beginning of the conversation."

"Please, everyone, stand up." Guruji said.

Paddy got his flute from his bag and started playing.

"Close your eyes and pay attention to the music. In your own time, I want you to sway and listen from your heart." Guruji said.

At first, I felt quite shy getting up and dancing with people around me that I barely knew, however, as I heard the notes of the basuri (flute) playing, the melody struck a chord in my being. I found myself automatically swaying from side to side, clicking my fingers rhythmically to the tune.

"What happened there?" Guruji asked.

"The music was so soothing," Naomi said.

Guruji said, "Did you find yourself feeling a little more connected? See this is how it is. Just like you can go into a home and, without anyone uttering a single word, you can feel the energy and sense if something is right or not!"

From Question to Quest

Lesson 4: Speech

"How pure is your speech? Your tongue has two purposes, it can create an oasis of harmony amongst chaos or it can be a razor sharp knife. Tell me how much control and skill do you use to speak kindly? Most of the things that come out of people's mouth are nonsense and you all engage in useless conversations."

Lesson 5: Smell

"You all are putting on perfume but after a while you cannot even smell your own perfume. It becomes a headache for those around you." Guruji said.

(People were giggling)

Lesson 6: Sight

"We experience the world through sight, but how much will you see? How many churches will you visit? After a while you don't even remember

Chapter 3

what you have seen. It's like watching so many movies. After a while all the stories get tangled up."

Lesson 7: Touch

"You have an obsession with sex (the mind is obsessed with it). Notice the men roaming around in nightclubs, see how dull they look; constantly thinking about sex."

"Within these six senses, you experience this world. Whilst they enable you to experience the world, note there are limitations to this experience. Any time you are stuck between for and against you are bound. Where is the freedom in this? You are burdened. When you are burdened, craving, and aversion arises and continues and there is no escape. This leaves impressions." Said Guruji.

"Impressions?" I asked.

"What do you mean by impressions?"

Guruji said, "You see, the mind is very sticky. Every event leaves an impression on our soul. It is like you placing your hand on some wet clay. The clay will mark your hand very easily. Anything we experience, we tend to label as pleasant, unpleasant, pleasure, pain, good, bad, happy, sad. So this leaves a memory within us.

These memories become your conditioning and this determines your behaviour, which then dictates your destiny. Impressions are deep, conditional experiences imprinted on the mind."

As Guruji spoke, all I could think of was the curd of guilt that was swallowing me up. How my life had turned out, how I was so caught up with my own marital upheaval that I didn't even get to say a proper goodbye to my best friend, my Baba. I was trying to let go but was chewing on this thought of remorse, feeling guilt and shame over and over again. 'Was I a fugitive running away from the shackles of my own past?' Another pointless thought entered my mind.

Guruji moved on and spoke about the seven layers of existence. He explained they are Body, Breath, Mind, Intellect, Memory, Ego and Self.

Chapter 3

The Seven Layers of Existence

The body is the physical vehicle that the soul adopts to carry out its plan. Remember that you are not your body. You have a body. Breath… breath is the connection between the body and the mind. Each emotion has a corresponding breath. For example, when you are scared or stressed how is the breath?" asked Guruji

"Shallow." I replied.

"Yes and how is it when you are relaxed and happy?" Guruji asked.

"Deep?" I said.

Everyone nodded.

"Many times you would have noticed that people ask you to take deep breaths if you are angry or panicked? This is because deep breathing releases stress and cools down the mind."

"How do you listen… how present are you? Is your mind flitting from the past to the future? This is the nature of the mind. The mind gallops towards the six senses. But let me ask you how much control of your mind do you have?"

"How do you bring the mind to the present?" Naomi asked.

"The secret lies in the breath. We will learn more about this later." Guruji said.

"Intellect… This is the rational mind. When you listen to anything, there is an inner dialogue in our minds that may say 'I don't like this, I don't agree with it,' or 'I like it, I agree' etc. This dialogue is nothing but the intellect, discriminating or judging."

"Memory… Memory is nothing but a storehouse of all the information you collate in your life; it has two parts—conscious and subconscious. Conscious memory remembers events, address, phone numbers etc. The subconscious is the one which stores all the impressions, unpleasant and pleasant outcomes, emotions etc. and this is the part that controls our behaviour."

"You mean this is the part that collects the events that we experience and controls how we interpret the events in our lives?" I asked.

Chapter 3

"Yes." Guruji replied.

"Ego… The ego is everything you identify with that is not your sacred self. Your ego is everything from your name, to your job title, to your possessions. The ego is a collection of ideas that make up your false identity. For example, I am what I have, I am what I do, I am what other people think of me."

"How you experience life depends on your inner world. You may be in the best of the outer world, living in luxury but if your inner world is disturbed, you will not be at peace."

"You need to take a look at your own thought patterns—there is a rhythm in them. And there is a rhythm in the consciousness."

"The 'self'; is the most subtle layer of existence is the self. The self shines through when you have dealt with Body-Breath-Mind-Intellect-Memory-Ego. A little bit of knowledge about these seven layers of existence makes a massive difference in our lives. It brings transformation." Guruji paused.

"Now, it is time for homework. Reflect on the following questions." Guruji said.

From Question to Quest

WHO ARE YOU?

WHAT DO YOU WANT?

HOW LONG DO YOU WANT TO BE HERE FOR?

Guruji finished the class with a simple, wind-down meditation and a chant of Namaste.

Chapter 3

Chapter 4

Healing the wounded heart

"Life is a mirror and will reflect back to the thinker what he thinks into it"

— *Ernest Holmes*

On the days that I wasn't on the happiness course or volunteering at Tumaini, I found myself strolling along Nyali Beach, an unspoilt oasis. Despite the heavenly scenery, my mind was still in a war of turmoil. I could not help but feel wounded that life had done me wrong and my marriage turned sour. I still found it so hard to accept how things had so suddenly changed.

I came in contact with a bitter taste of life's offerings and desperately searched for a way out. I remained hostage to the pain that tormented my heart, feeling powerless and fragile. When I married Raj, it was this feeling of perfection that we belonged together. A feeling of euphoria arose whilst we courted. That fate had chosen us to

Chapter 4

spend the rest of our lives together. At least that is how I was brought up to believe. Till death do us apart.

A year into the marriage, my mother-in-law was involved in a tragic car accident, leaving her disabled, which impinged on my time as I found myself taking care of her. The reality of daily married life was far from exciting and transitioned into a dull mundane reality. The newness quickly faded into the background and I started to notice Raj's flaws and became critical of his habits. Gradually, this started to eat away at me, corroding my enthusiasm.

Moments of resentment and bitterness emerged inside of me, anger for my unmet needs. My bitterness amplified. As time went by, Raj and I barely spoke to each other. To top it off, intimate times were a rarity. When we spoke, it would escalate into arguments, often turning into a bitter feud. My anger issues erupted inside of me and Raj became increasingly passive, withdrawing from me.

Consequently, he spent more time at work and travelling on business. Many times, I felt like we

From Question to Quest

had nothing in common and were coexisting in this institution called marriage. My emptiness of loneliness increased day by day. I didn't know how to be with the man I once loved so much. I didn't know how to move forward and face the humiliation that surrounded the possibility of divorce. I was afraid of letting my parents down and being stigmatized as a divorcee. At times we would look at one another trying to make it work, but deep down we both knew things were taking their toll.

I shared my marital issues with Guruji, hoping he could give me some clarity.

"I want to escape from my own self." I said, staring into space.

Guruji paused in his usual way.

"Before condemning others, first we need to look at ourselves. You want people to walk along the same track as you. The slightest change and you derail them out of your life. This is your botheration." Guruji said.

I stood stunned at what I had just heard. He paused again.

Chapter 4

"What energy have you been giving in your relationship?" He asked.

"I don't understand. What do you mean energy? I mean Raj is so unreasonable, he made me feel so empty." I said, balling my eyes out.

"He doesn't care for me anymore. The passion has gone. We don't connect the way we used to." I said in a shaky voice, trying to justify my dilemma.

"What intention are you bringing to the relationship?" Asked Guruji.

"You see, all relationships are mirrors of us. So everything you are feeling with Raj is a reflection of you inside. Isn't it so?" Guruji questioned.

I looked down, blankly staring at the floor, feeling ashamed. Somewhere along the way I knew that Guruji was right. I had to change, and the time was now.

"How should I move forward with Raj, Guruji? I can't possibly live alone. I am so scared."

"Seek the capacity to enjoy your own company. This can help you feel comfortable in your own

From Question to Quest

skin. The more you like your own company, the more capacity you will have to love someone. Only those who are capable of being alone can truly love someone. When you love someone, you accept them and focus on what you can give. They are your teacher and they are there for the time they are meant to be. You don't need to possess them. You don't need to be dependent on each other."

"What is the best thing to do Guruji?" I asked again.

"Listen to your heart. Ask the universe for guidance, and the answers will come and find you." He said.

"How do I do that?"

"Just ask. Say a prayer and ask. The universe can hear you if you are willing to listen." Guruji replied.

"In life, you have to take responsibility—we are all responsible for the thoughts, words and actions we bring into a relationship dynamic. You see, at a deeper level, we must be very conscious of our speech with the intention of doing no harm. The mind is fragile. It gets attracted to negativity so

Chapter 4

quickly, any small comment, of anything trivial people take to heart. People chew on it for years after, wounding themselves over and over again. The cycle of karma, cause and effect perpetuates itself, causing further troubles in the mind for this life and beyond."

I pondered on the guidance from Guruji, truly reflecting on his pearls of wisdom. I felt like I was waking up from my own destructive behaviours and shadows of insecurity. Only I didn't yet know how to change these unhealthy habits.

The next day I heard an inner voice talk to me.

'It is time to end the relationship with Raj. Let him go.'

This constant voice got louder and louder as I sat on a bench, staring at the clouds.

As life would have it, I randomly checked my emails when I returned to the hostel. To my surprise, I'd received an email from Raj.

This is what he'd written; 'Hey Maaya, I know that this is a cowardly way of communicating with you, but after all of the misunderstandings we have had, I thought writing to you would be the easiest way to tell you what I have been thinking.'

"Sorry for being a weakling! I will be on my way to start a new chapter in my life, in Australia, when you read this. I got a promotion as the Head of Commercial Bank in Melbourne. Maaya… you and I were only meant to be for this time. This was one chapter between us. You and I both know the dynamics between us have changed and we have grown apart. I want the best for you, and, despite our times of troubles, there have been some great moments. But this is where it has to end. Raj"

Stunned, I stared at the computer, my eyes gripping at the screen. I was only thinking about this yesterday. Perhaps this was a sign, but at the same time my heart was crippled.

I sat there sobbing for a good fifteen minutes until my tears dried up. What a day it had been; first the guidance from Guruji, and now Raj's email. My heartfelt bruised and I felt so helpless. Like a puppet on a stage, having little say in my life's direction. Deep inside I knew I had to let go, but the pain was crushing me inside.

Chapter 4

After moping about in my hostel for a few hours, I sat down, had a hot shower, and opened my notepad, attempting to do my homework. Who am I? I didn't know what to write. Notebook blank... I am Maaya.

Was I really just my nonsensical, countless thoughts that came gushing through my mind, making my head spin in circles? Was I my emotions that I was a slave to and felt I had no control over? Was I just a wife, daughter, PR Assistant? I felt like a failure. These questions baffled me and I didn't know how to respond to the questions. The more I thought about the questions, the more confusion arose.

What do I want? I want to feel like I was in the flow of life. I want to feel like life is happening for me and not to me. I wanted to have faith and trust and escape the crippling doubts in my mind.

I wanted to be happy. I want to heal from this grief. I wanted to escape the numbness and the dullness in my life. How long do I want to be here? Notepad blank... How long do I want to be here? What options were there?

From Question to Quest

The next day, Guruji asked, "So what did we learn yesterday?"

"I belong to you,." Naomi replied.

"So did you do your homework and reflect on the questions?"

"WHO ARE YOU? Are you your thoughts or even your emotions or maybe your feelings? Take a moment to think about this phenomenon. Who are you? WHAT DO YOU WANT? HOW LONG DO YOU WANT TO BE HERE FOR? Imagine if you have 10 days to live. How would you spend them? Think and ponder on it for a moment." Guruji said.

The room was silent with focused attention as we pondered and reflected as per Guruji's instruction.

"Here is another question: What does responsibility mean to you?"

We spent a couple of minutes reflecting on the question individually. As I was reflecting on this question, I noted that responsibility, to me, meant working and taking care of myself and being safe and. . .

Chapter 4

"RESPONSIBILITY IS THE ABILITY TO RESPOND in situations," Guruji interjected.

"How we respond to different situations that come our way; makes us very powerful. To claim your power, you must take responsibility," He continued. I suddenly saw this word with a new perspective. Oh my god, even when you break the word down you arrive at the ability to respond, I thought.

You see, when you adapt to different situations and can embrace any experience with confidence. A power inside of you emerges. Yes, we have responsibility. Family, work, household duties...but if situations are ever changing, the ability to respond to the changing situations reduces the conflict in us. The moment we struggle, conflict arises." Guruji said.

"Think about it..."

That night I reflected on my learning and noticed how resistant I was with most of the situations in my life. I feared change, and grumbled, and when things didn't turn to my liking I was often tempted to run away. This approach now needed to change.

From Question to Quest

Chapter 5

The profundity of serving others

"Only those who have learned the power of sincere and selfless contribution experience life's deepest joy: true fulfilment"
— *Tony Robbins*

As I stood at the gates of the Tumaini Home of Hope to start my volunteering work, I was warmly welcomed by Gill's staff.

Jamila, one of the staff members said, "You will be cleaning the toilets today." She directed me to the left wing of the orphanage.

"You are required to do this daily, and once you have cleaned the toilets in the morning, you can then move to the kitchen where you will help Amondi with the cooking. Is that okay for you?" I nodded and got started.

Chapter 5

A few minutes later, the influx of thoughts came flooding into my mind.

The stained walls were hard to scrub and I could feel myself getting frustrated as doubts erupted inside and I questioned what on earth I was doing here and why I was putting myself though this torture. But as usual I just didn't have the courage to say anything.

Two hours later, after cleaning the toilets I met Amondi, a timid 40-year-old Muslim man who cooked for the children. He instructed me to cut the vegetables. He was very jovial in nature, often cracking jokes. At 1pm the food was ready and the children arrived into the main hall to eat their food. I, along with the other volunteers, would help serve them their meals.

I met other volunteers. Guruji's assistant, Paddy Hogan, from Belfast, Northern Ireland was a 41-year-old life coach and yoga teacher. He was helping in the kitchen too. He was so friendly, and we ended up chatting about our lives and what had brought us here. Paddy appeared to be very grounded.

From Question to Quest

Paddy taught me the ropes of doing seva at Tumaini as I became familiar with the surroundings. I was trying my best to adjust to my new world. He took me around the classrooms where the kids were taught by volunteer teachers. Suddenly I got a flashback of my Baba teaching me from a red book with the timetables listed at the back, from when I was 10 years old.

I reminisced, I remembered sitting on the tattered chocolate colored sofa and with him, testing me on the equations, despite him being partly blind. 1 x 5 is? 3 x 5 is? 6 x 5 is? I heard his voice ringing in my mind. I really missed him.

I missed his wrinkly hands that felt like sandpaper; his wrinkled face that told a story of his own scars and his unspoken dreams. My hero. My Baba I sat there smiling at the kids remembering Baba.

The kids were so beautiful, kind and polite, despite their individual tormented pasts that had brought them to the orphanage. I learnt about Trudy, an 8-month-old baby who was abandoned on a roundabout.

Chapter 5

Jamie, one of the sisters told me "You know, when she came all of us went to church and prayed on our knees that she didn't have HIV. All we did was pray." Jamie said.

"She was a sick baby when she arrived, but our prayers healed her and she is perfectly healthy now." Said Jamie.

There was something so beautiful about Trudy. Babies were so present and free I reflected. I am sure I was like that once upon a time.

"These kids have had it tough." Paddy commented.

"Each one has had their own turbulent journey but you will never see it in their eyes. These kids are our teachers." Paddy said with conviction. "Their past can help us heal if we choose it too".

I sat there pondering on why these innocent children had to go through such turmoil so I asked Paddy.

"Why do you think the kids went through such atrocities?" I asked.

From Question to Quest

"I mean if there is really a God." I questioned.

Paddy interrupted, "Sometimes these answers are not so simple. Why something happens. Who deserves what, and why bad things happen to innocent lives is a very big question. I don't know the answer. I don't think anyone does. But what I can say is that in life, there are no accidents. Things happen for a reason.

If we think about our lives, we are a culmination of everything that has happened to us to, bring us to this very moment, then this moment is perfect. If we now try and reject something that happened in our past, we are simply going against the grain of the universe. Because you are the total sum of the parts.

So that means that everything that has happened to you today, pleasant or unpleasant brings you to the totality of your existence today. Like a flower. It is beautiful in its wholeness. You can dissect it to all the different parts.

The stalk, the stem, leaves, petals, but what gives the flower its beauty is the wholeness. Everything that happens in our lives brings people to their

Chapter 5

wholeness. There is a higher intelligence at play and the beauty and skill in life is to trust that intelligence." He said in a very grounded manner.

On a walk to the shops, while we were sipping on coffee, Paddy described how the happiness course had changed his life.

"I used to be so volatile before. Emotional rollercoaster was an understatement. Everything from, work, life, to relationships, juggling all the demands; I was desperately attempting to satisfy myself with the materialistic trappings, leaving an ever-increasing void on the inside. Most people do this you know. We think that we are going to experience the epitome of joy when we achieve something but it is an illusion. It is a fallacy. For years, I suffered from bouts of depression and negativity.

It took me a year before I could accept, I had some sort of mental health problem. Things just got worse. 3 years ago, I had a breakdown. Things got on top of me. That emptiness consumed me, eating me away. After a while you start to lower your expectations of life and accept mediocre. Sometimes I used to think, maybe this is all there is.

From Question to Quest

A mediocre existence. Time went by and my misery intensified, until one day I quit my work, and travelled to India to do some soul searching. I needed to change everything about my life. My health, my relationships, my work and how I was showing up."

"Welcome to my world, Paddy! I am not far from feeling dead inside you know! Lost is my middle name." I said.

"So, where did you go?" I asked.

"Well, I went to Rishikesh and spent a few weeks there. While travelling around I met a few kindred spirits and kept hearing about going to visit the Ashram in Bangalore. So off I went. Upon arriving at the Ashram, I met one of the Art of Living Teachers, Harry Valentine who recommended the happiness course. Meeting Guruji changed everything. His teachings of the Sudarshan kriya; have been like a lifejacket for me and they helped to keep the stresses at bay."

"Why do you think he is here?" I asked.

"He is here to help you meet yourself." Paddy replied.

Chapter 5

"What do you mean Paddy?" I asked, confused.

"You will see!"Paddy said vaguely.

"Since then, I have studied to be a life coach' and yoga teacher. I am deeply inspired to be on this path in helping people to carve out the best life possible. I help people play a bigger game in their life. I teach people how to make their life a living masterpiece." Paddy said confidently.

"How do you do that Paddy?" I asked inquisitively.

"I coach people in a number of areas of their life: health, wealth, relationships, career and contribution. It's very rewarding and fulfilling to empower other people to tap into their own power." Paddy said.

"You mean you coach them from where they are to where they want to be?" I asked.

"Exactly, I am the catalyst." Paddy replied.

"Well then I am curious Paddy. Or rather desperate! I need HELP! Do you think it would be possible for you to go through some coaching with me? I am like a lost goose right now." I said.

"Of course, we will talk more. Don't worry it's all happening perfectly." Paddy said, taking hold of my hand.

Paddy and I spoke non-stop for an hour, time simply flew by. It felt wonderful getting to know one another as we went grocery shopping for the seva day tomorrow. The conversation felt like a rude awakening to the fact that, perhaps, I needed to take more responsibility to cultivate my own life, rather than playing victim.

The next day was a big day for me. The Gayatri Mantra was playing in the Mandir. I closed my eyes, and took my attention to my heart while saying the following prayer in my head. 'Today is a very important day; it's a very precious day. I pray deeply that wherever my Baba is—that his wishes are fulfilled and I can do my seva from the heart today.'

Guruji was peacefully sitting in meditation with his eyes closed. A few minutes later he opened his eyes.

Chapter 5

"Guruji today is my seva day. I hope that my Baba receives this offering for that is why I am here Guruji." I said solemnly.

Guruji looked at me and remained silent.

He said very little, a man of few words, and stared at me with a sharp presence, then nodded. I wondered what he was thinking. I imagined he was thinking 'Poor broken girl, so entangled in her own crisis.'

After the class I went to the Nakumat (Tesco equivalent supermarket) to buy all the groceries. Back at the orphanage I assisted Amondi with making chips and a lentil curry. Naomi, Brendan, Kilna, Jenny and Paddy volunteered. I felt a connection with Naomi.

She was someone I wanted to be like; free and fearless, unlike me. I seemed to have an anchorless existence with little orientation, hoping I would find my way.

The day went smoothly and all the volunteers helped in the kitchen. By midday it was time to serve the food. As the kids arrived in the dining hall, Gill took them through a gratitude prayer. All

From Question to Quest

kids sat obediently around the table with their hands in a prayer position, eyes closed, and recited the prayer.

"We at Tumaini give thanks to the Lord to bring Maaya into our lives. She is an angel who has come to provide us with the food on the table today. Let us give thanks to the Father for the food that nourishes us today. Amen."

I began serving food to each child. Once all the kids had eaten, the volunteers helped themselves to lunch. One of the kids, Kimji sat on my lap whilst I happily fed him. He was eating so mindfully, with so much presence, focusing on every spoonful. He finished his plate and when he was served another plateful, his instant response was "WOW!" his eyes popped out and he grinned from cheek to cheek. No doubt he liked the attention, I thought.

Then it was time for ice cream. The kids were so excited. I really hadn't seen anything like it. You would not even think for a moment they were sick or scarred with a traumatic past. With such excitement, the whole meal was a great celebration. After the kids had eaten we took them to the garden to sing and play.

Chapter 5

As we were all playing in the play area, Kimji rushed over, gave me the tightest hug and said "Baba loves you."

I knelt down and asked him, "What did you say?"

"Your Baba loves you," he repeated.

As I heard this, my eyes started to well up. Kimji hugged me really tightly when he saw my teary eyes. How did he have any idea about my Baba I thought?

I asked him again, "What did you say?"

He said again, "Your Baba loves you!"

At this moment, I curiously wondered whether the seva had somehow fulfilled my Baba's wish. Naomi came to the play area, accompanied by a small poodle called Muffin. The dog was a 24 month old rescue which had been brought for the kids to play with. She was no doubt in her element, oozing with joy, as she was joined by her furry friend.

From Question to Quest

"Maaya come and play with Muffin!" she yelled across the play area, trying to get my attention!

"You know, until one has loved an animal, a part of one's soul remains unawakened. Dogs are simply unconditional. He reminds me of my fur baby, Romeo." Naomi said, tickling Muffin on his belly.

"How did you find Muffin?" I asked Naomi.

"Sad story, I found him dumped on the street only 8 weeks ago. Muffin was roaming around with a number of scars and looking helplessly frightened. I took him to the animal shelter and raised funds from back home so I could pay for all of his hospital care. I'm still on medication, but doing much better. You can see now that he is so much more playful. Animals are sentient beings."

"Sentient beings?" I asked.

"Yes, sentient beings; like humans. They have the capacity to feel pleasure and pain. Dogs, especially, feel emotions, like love and attachment! It's true what they say! Dogs are a man's best friend." Naomi said, grinning.

Chapter 5

Muffin continued playing with the kids, running around wagging his tail with such presence and play. He was simply in the moment.

"Dogs can teach us a lot of things about what matters in life. They don't want for much. My Romeo doesn't care whether you live in a mansion or a small shoebox. Whether you wear fancy clothes or not; a dog is the only thing on earth that will love you more than it loves itself. When I was so stressed with work Romeo saved me." She said softly, choking up.

"He simply understood and would often just lay by my side and look at me as if he was telling me it would all be ok. I love him—he is my soul. Dogs can teach us humans how to truly live."

"What do you mean?" I asked.

"If you and I have an argument; we are likely to hold on to the memory of it, possibly even for the next thirty years; whereas if you tell a dog off; in the next moment he will forgive and forget."

"It's sad really…how humans get so caught up with trivial things." I said.

From Question to Quest

"Yep." She agreed.

That night, as I entered my hostel room I decided to open the second scroll from Baba. Scroll number 2 read:

"Service to others is the rent you pay for the place you occupy here on Earth. Your life is not for you. It is for those around you."

As I fell asleep that night I remembered that Baba often used to say, giving opens the gateway for receiving. Our home was always open to strangers, as well as family. Despite his own troubles he never failed to give. I felt a sense of warmth inside my heart and called Maa to tell her about the seva day.

"Maaya, have you been reading the messages from your Baba?" She asked.

"Yes Maa and the irony is that whatever he is saying to me in the letter the same things are happening to me on the same day. Isn't it strange?" I commented.

"I am so pleased." Maa said.

Chapter 5

"I am feeling a little calmer in my mind. I have met this Guru by the name of Sri Sri Ravi Shankar and I am doing his happiness course. I am not sure where it will take me but I am trying to go with the flow." I said.

"Okay, stay safe. Be blessed." Maa said.

The next day, I spoke to Guruji about my seva day and shared with him what Kimji said. Guruji remained quiet for a few minutes, pondering on what I had told him.

"Guruji," I said.

"My father left a number of letters for me which I have been reading while I've been here. Last night, Baba told me in his letter that my life is not for me; it's for others around me. What did he mean by that? I don't fully understand." I asked.

"When you open your heart from a space of giving, rather than taking, then life can give you a new meaning. Any talents that you have been given, they are not for you, they are for others. If you are a musician, you play music for others. If you are a good cook, your cooking is for others." Guruji said.

From Question to Quest

"Know that you are here on Earth to give." Guruji answered.

"How do I remain in a space of giving Guruji?"

"Adopt the attitude of abundance. Notice how much the universe has given to you, there is so much abundance. Practice the skill of abundance and then grace will offer you more. This is how grace works." Guruji said.

Chapter 5

Chapter 6

Finding the divine in Yoga

"Yoga is the perfect opportunity to be curious about who you are."

— *Jason Crandell*

During our seva at Tumaini, Paddy and I spent time in deep conversation, talking about life and its ups and downs. As we began connecting with one another, I was in awe of his oozing passion for balance and his enthusiasm, which evoked a curiosity inside of me about the discipline of yoga.

Since my early teens, I had always suffered from lower back issues and as I had gotten older my back had got worse. I was taking pain suppressants to manage the pain and these tablets had become another part of my story. I wanted to feel the excitement that Paddy exuberated and I knew that if I continued being open, then perhaps I could change my reality.

"So, tell me more about Yoga," I asked Paddy.

Chapter 6

"Sure, would you like to know?" Paddy asked humorously.

"I mean, why is it so popular these days?"

"Because it's the medium that evokes healing on so many levels." Paddy replied.

"In what way?" I asked curiously.

"Let me give you a little background. The word, yoga, from the Sanskrit word 'yuj,' means to yoke or bind, and is often interpreted as 'union'. The Indian sage Patanjali is believed to have collated the practice of yoga into the 'Yoga Sutras' probably around 2,000 years ago. We are not mere physical bodies. There is so much more to us then we actually understand. We have a body, mind and spirit.

Yoga is the meeting of all these aspects of ourselves. Physical movement, or asanas, is a great way to release stale energy from the body. When there is balance, it enables the vital energy to flow. This flow of energy brings balance, spiritual insight, or siddhis, and helps us evolve spiritually. Remember Guruji talked about the impressions in your mind?"

From Question to Quest

"Yes, impressions." I repeated.

"Well, yoga is mentally scrubbing the garbage of our mind. Soul memory has been etched so deeply, ingrained into our existence that it takes many lifetimes to get rid of. We are talking many, many lifetimes of memories at a very deep level." Paddy emphasized.

"The first step is to strengthen our bodies. Through the practice of asanas, we can reduce stiffness, enabling the body to function at its optimum level. Strengthening the body is like kneading dough when making bread; it becomes transformed from a nebulous lump of unconscious flesh and bones into something that is full of life energy.

Scientists have researched how the practise of yoga activates the parasympathetic nervous system to reduce the fight or flight response which is an automatic physiological reaction that is activated under stress. Yoga is a complete science that unites the body, mind and spirit. It brings emotional integration and spiritual elevation, with a touch of mysticism.

Chapter 6

The second aspect in conjunction with the asana practise is made up of understanding that the mind is wavering. Always vacillating back to past events or looking ahead towards the future. Patanjali describes yoga as a practice that is able to still the oscillations of the mind." He paused, letting me absorb all that he was saying.

"So how do we bring the mind to some sort of stability when it is like a galloping horse that's Untamed?" He questioned.

"The breath." I replied.

"Correct!" Paddy said excitedly.

"Pranayama is the use of breath control, in a variety of ways, to purify the body and create free flowing energy. The secret of the breath has only been discovered by modern scientists today." Paddy claimed.

"Western science is now beginning to catch up with ancient eastern philosophy. The more control we have on our mind, the more power we have in our life. One of the most prominent researchers in the discipline of yoga is yoga practitioner, Dr

From Question to Quest

Khalsa, at Harvard Medical School, who speaks about the various components that make up yoga.

Mind-body awareness, breathing and relaxation techniques can change behaviours in a very positive way. Being able to control our stress response and the ability to observe the flow of thought, followed by moving into deeper states of meditation, can be transformative for people.

People are then inclined to gravitate towards positive goals to enhance life meaning and purpose. Dr Sarah Lazar of Harvard Medical School's research into yoga and meditation highlighted that those people that engaged in yogic practices that have insomnia, depression, anxiety, improve their ability to pay attention for longer.

She also found out that meditation helps with improving the grey matter in our brain which declines as we age."

After the brief conversation with Paddy about yoga I felt a curiosity in my soul. I was inquisitive to learn more. Could this be the medium to help me heal? What if I could heal my back troubles and

Chapter 6

could be free of medication? What if I could feel this sense of wholeness that Paddy exuberated?

The next day I decided to join an evening class at the orphanage where Kilna was teaching.

"Starting with three Om's; we begin the class." Kilna said, and we chanted the mantra in unison.

"Now, let us start with Savasana, lying on your back. Taking your attention into the present moment, letting go of all thoughts…be here right now…in this moment…Take a deep breath in, and breathe out. Nothing for you to do…simply observe the flow of thought…be a witness."

After 10 minutes we moved into warm up stretches.

"Okay. Now let us move on to Pavanmuktasana. Keeping the left leg straight, take a deep breath in and bring your right knee towards your chest. Release your lower back. As you breathe out, lift your nose to the knee."

A few minutes passed by and I noticed as I released my lower back; the stiffness in my body dissipated and a greater level of space was created.

From Question to Quest

I began learning to breathe into the pose. Just then Guruji walked in the room, observing our asana practise.

We turned our bodies to the right side and slowly came up into mountain position.

"Feel the connection between the four corners of the feet and the ground that is supporting you right in this moment." Kilna said.

"Tail bone is tucked under. Shoulders are relaxed and away from your ears, open your heart space. Standing tall… imagine you have a golden thread that is connecting the crown of your head up to the ceiling. Stand tall. This is Tadasana. Simply notice the connection between the body and the Mother Earth that is supporting you in this moment. A certain amount of steadiness in the pose is required. When you feel off balance, take your eyes and gaze to a point on the floor that isn't moving. This is the drishti point." Kilna demonstrated.

My mind was concentrating on the asana and the guidance from Kilna, but I observed so many thoughts ebbing and flowing. I was finding it hard to balance.

Chapter 6

"Notice what happens to the mind when you have your eye fixated on a defined point. Stop your eyes from moving."

Kilna came close to me to demonstrate.

"Good…very good Maaya." Kilna said.

I noticed in just 30 minutes of yoga asana that my body felt a little more stretched out with less aches and pains. Next was an easier pose, where we had to sit in a cross-legged position.

"Sitting down in Sukhasana with your spine upright. Allow the palms to softly rest on the knees, curling your fingers, and take your attention to your breath. Notice the incoming breath and the outgoing breath… and falling. Simply Let me walk you through this guiding meditation of learning to surrender." Kilna said in a mellow voice.

"The night comes and we give ourselves permission to dissolve, closing the ending of today as we enter ourselves into a rest of darkness. We let go of the valley we wish to cross in anticipation of our dreams, for a distance tomorrow. We allow ourselves the gift of rest, returning to the calmness of our breath…the silence of our mind."

From Question to Quest

"When we wake in the morning, as our eyes open, we slowly step into our mind's voice. We look outside, not realising that it is the same story we have identified with so much that it is our story that weighs us down. We walk invisibly, cocooned with all the things we wish to control, wishing life to be different.

We think, by keeping close to our worries and fears, we will have less of a chance for them coming true. When in fact the very act of doing so is causing us to live in the place we are trying to avoid. Surrender means to relinquish… to let go… What a beautifully divine word. We are not in control."

"We are floating on a cosmic river carried from the stars into the unknown. If we continuously release the need for controlling the flow of the river, we may just allow divine grace to enter our lives. The more we trust the journey the more fluid and joyful life becomes.The more we worry, the denser we become, weighing our hearts down like rocks that will sink deep into the ground.

Close your eyes, and take two deep breaths. Release a little more, sinking deeper and deeper

Chapter 6

into the earth. Notice how good it feels to be in your skin. Observe any tension in your body, neck, shoulders and fill your lungs.

Let all the tension go. Bring yourself gradually back into the environment, noticing the sounds near and far. Gradually moving your toes and fingers. When you are ready you can open your eyes."

"Namaste."

After the meditation session ended, I knew in my heart that this was me opening up and learning to surrender. I remained cradled in a state of grace. A new chapter awaited, and I felt like I was trying to learn to trust, whatever that meant!

From Question to Quest

Chapter 7

My life, my responsibility

"When you change the way you look at things, the things you look at change"

— *Wayne Dyer*

As time went by, I adjusted to the routine of serving at Tumaini after attending the course with Guruji. Paddy, Brendan, Kilna, Jenny, Naomi and I all became good friends sharing stories of our journeys as well as the happy and uncomfortable moments.

My seva at Tumaini of cleaning the toilets was something I was beginning to adapt to and what began with a disgruntled attitude now became a daily routine. I enjoyed helping Amondhi in the kitchen and sharing ideas of what other dishes we could serve the kids. Moreover, Paddy was coaching me and I started to experiment with yoga when I felt anxious; which was most of the time.

Chapter 7

As I started to practice the stretches, aches and pains combined with the stiffness stored in my body would subside. Since Baba's passing, broken sleep was the norm, but the guided meditations were helping me sleep better. Becoming conscious of my breath enabled me to learn to let go of the tensions and thoughts.

That afternoon, I went to the Zikhina café near Nyali beach to meet Paddy for my coaching session. The weather was a warm 25 degrees and most people were out relaxing on the beach.

"Maaya," Paddy said,

"Are you ready to change your life and take it to another level?" I looked at Paddy and remained quiet for a moment,

"Are you seriously ready?" he asked excitedly.

"I think so," I replied cautiously.

"My life is a mess. I need to change things," I said Paddy.

"So, coaching is for people who want to get the most out of life and play a bigger game. In order to make a start, you need a journal. You need to keep an open mind as some aspects of coaching will take you to uncomfortable places."

"Are you ready for this discomfort?" Paddy said.

"I am ready," I said to Paddy.

Paddy opened his bag, took out a journal that read 'be your own kind of beautiful'.

"Here you go." Paddy said, handing me the pad.

"Let's begin; have you ever wondered what makes successful people successful? I mean they don't just get lucky you know!"

"We are creatures of habit. They have habits in place which they practise daily."

Paddy continued, "Extraordinary people operate on a higher level. They have a well-crafted vision of their life and they then implement the systems and processes to help them achieve their dreams."

"Yes," I said, nodding.

"If you could do anything... What would it be?" Paddy asked.

Chapter 7

"Most people spend their lives exhausted, too busy focusing on low priority tasks. They dabble in major things. Dabbling simply scratches the surface but remember if you really want to become a master at something, you have to master the craft and this takes skill, habits and continuous practise."

"I have taught life mastery sessions for five years now. I teach all over the world. Sadly, the formula to go to college, get a degree, fall in love, get married, have children often doesn't work, hence the reason why many of us are so empty and unfulfilled…"

"And just in case you are wondering if it is possible to have optimum health and energy, emotional balance, spiritual fulfilment, mental wellbeing, develop a great relationship and be abundantly rich, I am here to tell you… YES, it is possible. There is a system for doing it. Once you understand the mechanics… you can cultivate your best life."

"I am ready," I said, lifting my posture and firmly standing upright.

From Question to Quest

"I want to change Paddy," I said.

"The first component of life mastery is HEALTH and FITNESS. It was the Dalai Lama who said, 'it is man who sacrifices his health to make money and then uses his money to recuperate his health'."

"This is the ONE AREA that is intimately connected to every other area."

"So, I want to ask you — what do you put in your body? Why does health and fitness matter to you? Moreover how do you use your body?"

"At work, over 3 billion dollars are spent on work-related stress. Thirty percent of the world's population are overweight. Think about our lifestyle today. We live in boxy houses with congested space. We travel in a box; we are glued to a box. We have lunch from a box. Ninety-five percent of health and disease prevention in our bodies is in our control if we change our diet and lifestyle."

"So I want you to ponder on these questions."

"What are your thoughts about your body?"

Chapter 7

"How would you rate the current health and fitness levels?"

I realised that up until now, I had not thought very positively about my body. Rather that I was very harsh in criticising my body. I realised that my thoughts about myself were very critical, often self-sabotaging.

"Where did these thoughts come from?"

Paddy replied, "A combination of your own memories and your upbringing. Do you remember Guruji spoke about impressions? Well these are the impressions that have been imprinted in your mind and are impacting your behaviour."

"So how do I change my thoughts about my body?" I said.

"Identify an affirmation. An affirmation is a positive statement that you are willing to recite daily. For me, 'I have a youthful energetic body'. As you recite positive statements, they become ingrained in your nervous system." Paddy replied.

"Paddy, sometimes I feel like I don't matter." I said.

From Question to Quest

Paddy replied, "Do you know Maaya, a butterfly flapping its wings in New Mexico has the power to cause a hurricane in China. A single action could cause a reaction on the other side of the world. Don't underestimate the power of who, you are and how you can contribute for the betterment of others."

"Either you break down and give up or we break through the mud. The choice is yours." Paddy said

"The mud I asked?" looking puzzled.

Paddy elaborated, "Imagine that you are a lotus seed buried beneath a muddy lotus pond. With a determined heart, you begin to wiggle in the earth. You grow roots deep, deep into the mud. Your little stem grows up slowly. Suddenly, 'pop' you are out of the mud! Your stem grows higher and higher, taller and taller. You rise up slowly, fighting against the muddy water. All of a sudden, you are out of the muddy pond! You reach up towards the warm sun, shining down on you."

"Your lotus bud begins to grow on top of your stem. It expands and grows larger and larger, finally bursting into full bloom; a white lotus

Chapter 7

flower. You stand beautifully above the muddy water, not dirtied by the mud from which you grew. My invitation to you is to grow out of the muddy pond."

"When I look at you I see a mirror of who I was not so long ago. There is so much potential waiting to…"

"I feel like a failure," I interrupted.

"Where is your focus?" Paddy said challengingly.

"At the moment you're feeling hurt. I understand your relationship has broken down. You lost your loving father, and I am not trying to undermine this Maaya."

"But you can't control EVERYTHING."

"It's your choice, you either stay in the hurt or you create some meaning out of what has happened!"

"DECIDE IT IS THAT SIMPLE."

"What do you really want in your life?"

From Question to Quest

"Everyone is here for a reason... What are you here to become?"

"What will you focus on NOW! How can you create some positive meaning about the events in your life? There is a grand design YOU MUST BELIEVE THIS."Paddy said.

"Okay, okay, okay so how do I know what I am meant to be doing here?"I asked.

"I challenge you to listen carefully to the whisper of your heart."

"The whisper of the heart is a gradual awakening that taps into your spirit waiting to unfold. Every day you have to be ready to hear the song inside your heart. It's a very subtle whisper.

You have to be ready to listen to the gradual murmur in your heart. No one suddenly wakes up and finds their wave of inspiration you know. Life and dreams don't work like that. The universe buries jewels deep within us all, and then stands back to see if we can find them."

"Lie down and look up at the sky. What do you see?"

Chapter 7

"The sky… the clouds," I replied.

"Okay fixate your eyes on a cloud. Take a deep breath."

"Keep looking at that cloud. Keep looking at it until I say stop."

"Now blink. What have you noticed?" Paddy asked.

"The cloud is moving." I replied.

"What else?" Paddy asked.

"The shape changed." I replied.

"Exactly… each and every moment everything is changing. Holding on to a moment is stifling. You can't hold onto anything around here."Paddy advised.

"You mean to say I don't have any control right Paddy?" I asked.

"No, what I am saying is that if we focus on our internal state of being then. Then this is something we can control. Our experiences that happen… they happen… Often inevitably it happens to help us to grow and expand. But we can choose to create meaning out of the most difficult times. Most of us are so focused on fixing the outer world that nothing changes. Then we wonder why we are still running on empty."

"Your internal world, your attitude, your ability to let go to be flexible is what we have control over."

"I understand that 97% of blame can be placed on Raj! But what about the 3% of the part you played. What part did you play, and how are you taking responsibility?"

"It's fundamental to know this otherwise you will repeat the same mistakes in your next relationship. These patterns are buried deep inside of us and until we don't bring them to our consciousness, they will keep repeating themselves. Trust me, I have been there. So, while you are enduring this excruciating pain right now in your heart… The pain that never seems to want to leave… The agonizing heartbreak that has invaded your safety… My question to you is how can you come from a space of forgiveness and love and what would this bring you?"

Chapter 7

I was silent so he continued.

"See most people have animosity and hatred amongst painful breakups. I get it. Someone has to be blamed for your upheaval. After all, the trauma is for real. But what if there was a different way. Another paradigm… Would you be willing to consider it?"

"I think so." I said.

"Take responsibility. We are responsible for the thoughts, words and actions we bring into the relationship dynamic. At a deeper level, we must be very conscious of our speech with the intention of doing no harm. The mind is fragile. Gets attracted to negativity so quickly… Any small comment about anything, often things that are trivial, people take to heart. People chew on it, sometimes for years after, wounding themselves over and over again. The cycle of karma, cause and effect perpetuates itself.

The karmic connection ceases to end, causing further troubles in the mind for this life and beyond. Ponder on this! I know it isn't easy. It's getting late so I am going to give you some work to do. Write down all your frustrations about Raj, everything, on a piece of paper. All your frustrations…let it all out and bring the piece of paper with you when we meet at the BBQ in 3 days. You're not going to send it to him, don't worry." Paddy said reassuringly.

"We will leave it at that. We will do more coaching before the BBQ."

Paddy took hold of my hand and said "I know this is painful and I know you are in pain. But you are on your way to heal and the path is unfolding beautifully. Just trust me on this, okay?"

I headed back to my hostel to spend some time reflecting on the questions. My mind is my greatest asset. I wrote my life vision:

- I want optimum physical health where I have energy to enjoy my life at every level. I want to heal my back issues and do the things I have not yet done, explore the world, travel to a few places and feel comfortable in my skin.

- I want to be thriving in my relationships.

Chapter 7

- I want to work in a role where I feel empowered, I want to find my passion in a role where I could help people. Make a difference.

From Question to Quest

Chapter 8.1

A Paradigm shift

"Knowing others is intelligence; knowing yourself is true wisdom. Mastering others is strength; mastering yourself is true power."

—Lao Tzu

I plucked up the courage to put pen to paper and wrote a letter to Raj, as Paddy had suggested. I ended up writing five pages of all my buried resentments that festered inside of me for years. Raj and I had a way of covering things up, rather than talking about the issues that arose.

Paradoxically so much was left unsaid and at times too much was already spoken to create the estrangement. The emotional residue translated from my heart into the notepad as I wrote away. At the end of the experience, my whole body ached from emotional fatigue. My heart was on fire. I was so exhausted and I wanted to disappear.

Chapter 8.1

On Friday, I met Paddy just before the BBQ. I was eager to unravel some further learning, but apprehensive as to what was coming next in my coaching session.

"So, how did you find the session? What reflections have you come up with?" Paddy asked.

"I have been doing a lot of thinking Paddy," I said.

"I am determined more than ever to transform my life. I want to create meaning in my life and make an impact."

"Excellent. This is great to hear and only the beginning. We will be putting systems in place to crystallize this vision into reality. Stay with me, okay?" He said.

Paddy had taken my hand in his as we walked towards the fire.

"Are you ready?" He asked, I shrugged my shoulders, I didn't know what was coming.

From Question to Quest

He said, "It's time to liberate yourself and find your true power. This is YOUR step towards emotional freedom. OWN IT!"

I threw the letters into the fire and noticed the extreme tension in my body gradually dissolve.

After staring in space for 10 minutes, I said, "I reflected on what you said earlier today Paddy! I have contributed to the way I was showing up in this partnership with Raj. I can't blame it all on him. It was me. The criticisms, the desperate yearning to be heard and seen…I am willing to take responsibility for my role in the break up. I am going to make an unwavering commitment to myself."

"Good to hear." Paddy said.

"Paddy what was the significance of burning the letters then? I don't understand." I asked.

"Remember we are creatures of habit. All our experiences have an emotional charge attached to them. When you burn the paper, you transform the emotion from the subconscious to the conscious… which brings healing. Think in terms of energy frequency and vibration. My question to you is

Chapter 8.1

this. Can you make a paradigm shift on how you see this chapter of your life that is changing form?

A chapter that will now propel you into another dimension of awakening... If you were able to shift what impact would this be on your quality of awareness? Think! Don't answer the questions. Simply ponder." Paddy said.

"How should I be showing up in relationships, Paddy? I have reflected from your guidance and I feel like I am waking up from my own destructive behaviours and shadows of insecurity."

"Replace criticism for appreciation. Criticism attacks the core of a person's character. People like to be accepted for who they are."

Silence prevailed for a good few minutes, and I stared into the fire.

"Let me share with you how the universe works." Paddy offered.

"Did you know that quantum physicists have discovered that physical atoms are made up of a whirlpool of energy that is constantly spinning and vibrating, each one radiating its own unique energy signature? Therefore, if we really want to observe ourselves and find out what we are, we need to perceive ourselves as energy and vibration, radiating our own unique frequency.

This is fact and is what quantum physics has shown us time and time again. We are much more than what we perceive ourselves to be, and it's time we began to see ourselves in that light. If you observed the composition of an atom with a microscope you would see protons, neutrons and electrons, which make up the structure of an atom. As you focused in closer and closer on the structure of the atom, you would see nothing, you would observe a physical void..." Paddy paused.

"You look perplexed."

"I am... I mean..." I stuttered.

Paddy interrupted, "I know what you are thinking. What does this have to do with mastering your life? Well, feelings, thoughts, and emotions play a vital role. Quantum physics helps us see the significance of how we all feel. If all of us are in a peaceful loving state inside, it will no doubt impact

Chapter 8.1

the external world around us, and influence how others feel as well.

So you need to think in terms of energy, frequency and vibration. Let me explain a little more. In simple terms, your thoughts matter, really matter. Dr Masaru Emoto, a Japanese scientist and water researcher, discovered how thoughts and vibrations affect the molecular structure of water. So how can you be aware of your thoughts? What has Guruji been teaching you?!" Paddy quizzed.

"Simply noticing and becoming aware." I said.

"Exactly! The first way to fix any problem is AWARENESS. Simply notice what is going on so you can pinpoint it, and know what you want to change. Many of us feel like our brain is an endless chatterbox machine with no pause, mute, or off switch. Our lives don't have to be lived this way. Start to be mindful of your thoughts on a daily basis.

If something negative comes up, notice it, allow it to rise to the surface, maybe ponder on it for a short time, and then let it go. Think of this as taking an inventory of your thoughts, so you can really get a grasp of what goes on in that head of yours on a daily basis.

Once you know what really goes on in your mind, you can cultivate the tools necessary to settle it down a bit. Repeat a mantra or affirmation, focus on your breath, or go for a walk. These are all things you can incorporate to bring your mind back to the now, and out of a negative spin."

Chapter 8.1

Chapter 8.2

The hidden jewels

"We don't realize that, somewhere within us all, there does exist a supreme self who is eternally at peace."
— *Elizabeth Gilbert*

Guruji was teaching yoga and meditation from a tender age, but it was during a 10-day silence in Shimoga, India that the Sudarshan Kriya was born. Sudarshan Kriya is a cleansing technique that incorporates specific natural rhythms of the breath which harmonizes the body, mind and emotions.

Su means proper and darshan means vision. Kriya is a purifying action. Through specific actions of the breath during the Sudarshan Kriya we are able to experience our own nature, our being.

Over 70 independent studies conducted have demonstrated a comprehensive range of benefits from practicing the Sudarshan Kriya to harmonize the whole system and eliminate the accumulated stresses stored in the body. Millions of people from

Chapter 8.2

all walks of life have been touched by the healing power of the Sudarshan Kriya; Villagers, corporate employees, housewives, teenagers, trauma victims, soldiers, business leaders, prisoners, university students. People across all continents have found the benefits of this powerful breathing technique.

"Let us sit comfortably, spine upright, shoulders relaxed." Guruji said, guiding us through the Kriya, alongside Paddy, who was assisting.

After doing Kriya, time vanished, I became thoughtless. My body became electrically hot and I felt like I was floating, I could feel the kundalini energy rise from the bottom of my spine to the top of my head. I felt like someone had washed my mind of the entire emotional residue that had been weighing me down for years. The passing of time subsided. When I opened my eyes, moved around, and stretched my body my back pain was no longer there. It had vanished…A miracle…

"Guruji, what is this experience?" I asked.

"This is samadi. A few precious moments where you notice the cosmos; I could see the whole of the cosmos. The electric blue stardust that flickered radiantly; it is the highest point of stillness. No thought, no mind, just stillness." Guruji said.

I sat there in amazement.

"Everything in this universe is dynamic. This whole consciousness is one dynamic energetic pulse. I am now going to teach you how to elevate your consciousness. How do you turn your pain into power? Are you ready to learn the secret treasures?" Guruji asked.

I nodded excitedly still feeling the effervescent feeling of the blissed-out Kriya experience.

"Remember one thing, the purpose of pain is to propel you into taking action. It is not to make you suffer." Guruji advised.

"The first treasure is Santosha-contentment. Being happy with what you have takes a little skill. If one is unhappy, even in the best of situations… Even in paradise, you will be grumbling. When you are happy… What is happening? Relaxation in the mind... When the mind is relaxed the joy within us expands. There is a flow in life, rather than an uphill struggle.

Chapter 8.2

"How do we practise contentment Guruji?" I asked.

"Simply adopting the attitude of choosing to be happy, come what may. Don't let your smile be shaken. What is there to be unhappy about when everything is changing? Trying to control the outer world when everything is so ephemeral is like holding onto a cloud that is passing by... It is pointless."

Paddy spoke of his time when he had the opportunity to meet Nick who was born without limbs and now worked all over the world inspiring others.

He told me, "Either I can be very angry at God or thankful. I decided to be the miracle to help make the world a better place."

I could not change my circumstances. I had so many questions and yet I had no answers. Everyone in the room welled up as they listened to Nick's heartfelt story. I felt like someone had ignited the valour in me to wake up.

"Some homework for you is to write down all the things that you are grateful for in the next 40 days and see how it can help you shift your focus." Paddy said, handing out notepads.

Guruji continued, "The second treasure is service. Seva is a Sanskrit word meaning selfless service. Giving yourself, your talents, your labours, your time to uplift others without any expectations whatsoever. By selflessly serving others you inculcate humility in yourself and merge with the divine."

"Seva is the single most powerful purifying agent of life mastery. The meaning of service is doing something without any expectation whatsoever. We live as though life owes us something. We expect from our spouse, parents, friends, family and acquaintances and when they don't meet our expectations we are stunned with this behaviour. Yet, how frequently do we observe our behaviour?"

"We bypass our shortcomings so quickly, yet when someone lets us down, we are very reluctant to forget this. In fact we hold onto it for too long. Let me tell you, there is no greater calling than to serve others. Service enables you to step out of

Chapter 8.2

your own little bubble. Your problems that bottle you up subside and trivialities fade away.

Have you noticed how useful a tree is? A tree gives oxygen. It is a place for birds to live. It never causes pollution. You can build a home with a tree. Man is so destructive and is alive and useless as a corpse. Service, therefore, should be your breath!"

"The third treasure is faith. Faith is a wealth that keeps your mind centred and intact. It evokes such a quality in your awareness, helping you to pursue your life with stability."

"Yes challenges will arise, and you may question your faith, but eventually you will come back to your faith. There is a power bigger than you to deal with your problems. As time goes by you will be able to see the bigger picture, connecting the dots, and when you can see this broader perspective, your faith continues to renew."

"The fourth treasure is surrender. It is when we surrender with a state of wonder that we enter into a realm of tranquility. This is where miracles happen. People believe that surrender is a sign of weakness… for the feeble... Let me tell you it's the other way around. You do your best and then leave the rest to a higher power. This does not mean adopting a passive attitude. I do nothing now.

I surrender everything to God. This is about you playing your part, being dynamic and making an effort. But after you have done what is needed, it is time to surrender. When every door closes, that is the time to let go! This is not the ending… it is simply the beginning."

After Guruji spoke about the four secret treasures, I found myself in deep contemplation, soaking up the wisdom that I just learnt. The session ended with a 10 minutes meditation which I found blissful. I could not help but smile. The notion of surrender was reiterated to me time and time again.

My mind felt a lot more serene and a lot more stable. In my heart, I experienced a paradigm shift from the minutia of life's trivialities to an expansion in knowing and trusting that there was a higher order to the universe.

Chapter 8.2

From Question to Quest

Chapter 9

The love that you seek

"Learn to get in touch with the silence within yourself and know that everything in life has a purpose."
—*Elizabeth Kubler Ross*

The final day of the happiness course felt like the start of a beautiful sacred chapter to how life could be. I now felt like a flower about to blossom into a full bloom. The ambience in the room was hard to describe, people smiling and uplifted. Completely different to when we had first started the course. It was like there was intuitive lightness in the atmosphere.

I was practising my Kriya and yoga daily before volunteering at Tumaini now. Somewhere along this journey I had begun to see with new eyes. With a sharper vision, from a broader perspective; I was healing, feeling stronger and I had a surge of enthusiasm for my next chapter in life. I wondered

Chapter 9

what was next. I felt a level of excitement I had not experienced in a long time.

Paddy took us through some yoga Asanas emphasising the breath as a way of healing the body. Releasing the tension, followed by Kriya. Once again, my body felt at ease as I practised yoga, and Kriya was like going into a washing machine and scrubbing the stains from my mind.

Gradually I was learning about how changing the rhythm of the breath affected the state of my mind. After one-and-a-half hours of practise, people were smiling and bathing in their own juice of serenity. Guruji arrived in the hall and sat down, pausing…

"Something gets spoilt when words are spoken." Guruji said softly.

"Ninety percent of people do not like being by themselves…They are scared of being alone, but I tell you, it is in silence that one gets to meet with their true spirit."

Guruji was emanating in love and tranquility and I wanted to emulate his vibration. He spoke with with such presence and focus. Silence is an opportunity for you to go within. It is like fine tuning the radio station.

"Observing the scattered mind, reflecting and introspecting on your life gives you the power to gain such clarity. This is where the power is. The power of creativity, of genius, lies in silence." Guruji continued.

"We will now step into silence for 24 hours with no contact with anyone else. Phones switched off. No conversation allowed. Simply being in your own company... Simply observing." Everyone sat quietly contemplating the instruction from Guruji.

"No pleasantries with anyone needed. No 'thank you' and 'please', no 'sorry' needed. Which you often don't mean anyway" Guruji smirked in a jovial way.

"Simply drop all your obligations."

The group giggled and then we got ready.

Silence commenced.

As soon as I heard this instruction, in a blink of an eye, my logical mind stepped in to cause havoc

Chapter 9

and the tiny ounce of serenity that I contained inside of me over the last few days quickly dissipated. I had never spent time alone doing nothing. I resisted my own company. Daunted, impervious to my experience, I felt disgruntled.

The passage of time dragged slowly. I didn't know what to do with myself... how to be with myself. The deprecating thoughts came flooding back like an intruder, swallowing me up again. At times dormant. At times raging... A spectrum of emotions escalated through my being, I had no clue whether I was coming or going.

Fear haunted me, knocking on my chest cavity and heavily suffocating me, squeezing the air from my lungs. My rib cage tightened and I struggled to breathe. I silently muttered to myself trying to escape the fear.

How can someone just die in a flash like that? The question was rewinding in my mind and I pondered over and over again. I was still mourning for Baba's passing.

My grief was bleeding and I didn't know what to do. As I pushed my thoughts aside they magnified.

From Question to Quest

Countless moments of frustration, anger and irritation submerged in my mind. I really didn't know what the point of this silence process was and I felt increasingly agitated. So the myriad of endless thoughts continued. The thought factory just kept producing thoughts.

Most of which were nonsense. I found myself resisting more and more. The minute I tried to bring my mind into some order the influx of thoughts battled with me and won.

I found myself increasingly frustrated with no control over my mind and its constant chatter. I felt fed up. I wanted to leave and run away. I didn't want to be sitting in some lonesome silent monastery. Observing the moment fully, my mind, the untamed horse calmed down. The minute that I fully accepted the moment, my mind calmed down.

I took a deep breath and exhaled loudly. I gave in completely and let everything erupt inside my head. The moment I fully accepted myself in this space my mind calmed down.

Chapter 9

Gradually, a period of quietness transcended inside and my mind became calmer. The more I accepted the present moment, the more I became one with it. Later on that day, I was seated on a beach right in front of Nyali beach. The sky was a crystal-clear blue with the white horizon of clouds descending behind the mountains. At this precise moment in time, I was observing the beauty and I was in awe of it.

I was surrounded by rugged hills with distinctive carvings and a line of lush green trees. In the distance I saw beautiful mountains standing tall, with prominent pinnacles of snowflakes draped over them. I was all alone and yet nature — the water, the breeze, the sunlight became an extension of myself and I felt at one with the universe.

The more I embraced the present moment the more I became one with it. I began to experience a glimmer of ecstasy. Joy was rising in me and my heart started to sway. I counted my blessings and bowed to the sunshine as I soaked up the cosmic energy.

I felt so blessed.

From Question to Quest

I reflected back on the conversation with Paddy about the theory of wholeness and started to see the meaning behind the events in my life. The next day we all arrived back in the mandir.

Guruji asked, "How have you found being with yourself? If it has been frustrating and irritating… That is fine."

"If it has been a fun experience that is also fine… Whatever you found… All is okay here." He said kindly.

"What we will do now is our last meditation then you can break your silence."

Everyone sat attentively reflectively looking and listening to Guruji as he spoke. The atmosphere was distinctive and serene. Everyone's faces looked fresh and renewed. Another meditation session felt like I had cleared out another layer of past impressions that no longer served me.

It was time to break the silence.

"Who would like to go first? How has this experience been for you?" Guruji asked.

Chapter 9

"Calm." Brendan replied.

"Cleansed," I replied.

"Reborn." I murmured.

"Remember who you are? 'Sat Chit Ananda'," Guruji explained.

"'Sat' means Truth. There is a part of you that never changes. Your ego, personality, beliefs may change over time but there is something in you that is magnanimous. This luminous mystery that you are a part of never changes.

'Chit' means consciousness—that part of you that is aware. 'Ananda' means bliss. Silence brings you to another depth of consciousness. It is only in silence, and when the mind is somehow settled that you can see your own reflection. We cannot see our reflection in running water."

"You know in the Gita, it is Krishna who said to Arjuna, 'When a person experiences pleasure or pain. These experiences are fleeting; they come and go. Bear them patiently Arjuna.' Only in silence can you lift the veil and get in touch with who you are. Become a witness.

From Question to Quest

Outside situations cannot touch you. If you reflect on past challenges, past events, and situations that have happened; whether they have been pleasant or unpleasant, where are they now? They have all gone. You are untouched. There is no insurmountable difficulty before a brave man." Guruji said.

Chapter 9

From Question to Quest

Chapter 10

The power of surrender

"Surrender is a journey from the outer turmoil to inner peace."

— **Sri Chinmoy**

On Saturday, Paddy, Brendan, Naomi, Kilna, Jenny, and I decided to hire a car and drive to Wisini Island. Wisini Island lies in Southeast Kenya, 3 kilometers off the coast of the Indian Ocean and 75 kilometers South of Mombasa.

Paddy had organised the road trip after meeting the tour guide, Ali Baba, whilst Paddy was teaching yoga. Ali Baba picked us up in his car and we were all excited to explore this island and venture out.

As we arrived at his house, we were greeted by his wife, Shamu, and their 8-year-old daughter,

Chapter 10

Amadi. They were so overjoyed to see guests at their door. The house was beyond basic. The dusty pink walls looked dated and had sporadic marks dotted on them. The torn curtains were loosely hanging and a small electric light bulb barely lit up the house.

Despite the modest living conditions, there was no shortage of love here. Ali Baba's family were in awe, greeting guests as they arrived, smiling and welcoming everyone into their home.

Shamu lit a candle and recited a prayer.

"We thank the Lord Jesus Christ and ask that he bless this food and bless the people that have come to eat with us today." We held hands and ended the prayer with Amen.

Shamu made the most mouth-watering dishes; delicious aromatic cumin rice with barbequed Aubergine curry.

I felt an immediate belonging and connection here. We ate, laughing and chatted in 35 degree humidity, with no air conditioning and house flies buzzing around. But the warmth and smiles filled the atmosphere in Ali Baba's home.

From Question to Quest

We happily embraced the moments fully. I made friends with Amadi, as I braided her chestnut coloured hair, just like Maa used to do with mine when I was a child. The evening was wonderful, but among the chattering and eating I had noticed a slightly subdued look on Shamu's face and intuitively knew something wasn't right. After dinner, the whole neighbourhood, which only consisted of 5 other families that lived on the island, came over to huddle together and watch TV.

"This house belongs to everyone on the island." Said Shamu.

At 9.30pm, my travel companions decided to go night fishing while I decided to spend the evening with Shamu and Amadi. Amadi's face lit up when she knew I was staying behind, she wanted me to tell her a story. After reading to her, Shamu tucked Amadi in bed. Shamu shared with me her tear-jerking story. How Ali Baba's struggled to provide for the family, with no job for over a year and how they almost lost their home.

"It was very difficult; I cried a lot on how we would survive but God has been so kind. We now

Chapter 10

have steady people like you coming to visit the Island and we are so grateful. God tests us in life." Shamu said looking into my eyes.

She started to well up. As we continued talking; Shamu looked sombre.

"What's the matter Shamu?" I asked.

"I have been asked to go to the hospital tomorrow to investigate a possible cancer in my cervix. Sorry if I have not been completely myself. I keep thinking about it, wondering what will happen to my baby girl..." Shamu replied, unable to finish her last sentence.

"Shamu, I am going to come with you to the hospital." I said holding her hand.

Shamu burst into floods of tears.

"Just when you think everything is going to be okay, troubled waters are just a moment away. I am sure the Lord knows best, but Amadi is so young. She needs me."

"Shamu," I said, holding her hand tight.

From Question to Quest

"Nothing will happen. It is better to have an investigation right now so the right treatment can be given."

I barely slept that night. I was munched on by house flies and felt on edge, pondering how Shamu's investigation would go today. Once we arrived at the hospital. The nervousness on her face spoke a thousand words as we waited to be called.

Shamu said, "Let's read the Bible and pray to Jesus," as she took the Bible out of her handbag.

Shamu started to read Psalm 23 from the Bible,

"The LORD is my shepherd, I lack nothing. He makes me lie down in green pastures, he leads me beside quiet waters, he refreshes my soul. He guides me along the right paths for his name's sake. Even though I walk through the darkest valley, I will fear no evil, for you are with me; your rod and your staff, they comfort me. You prepare a table before me in the presence of my enemies. You anoint my head with oil; my cup overflows. Surely your goodness and love will follow me all the days of my life, and I will dwell in the house of the LORD forever."

Chapter 10

Fifteen minutes later, the consultant Gynecologist called Shamu into the theatre. I hugged her tightly to reassure her she wasn't alone. She was trembling,

"You are going to be fine." I said.

"Yes." She replied,

"Jesus is by my side. He will take care of me." She said, apprehensively gazing at the floor.

I sat outside the theatre contemplating, astonished at Shamu's depth of faith. Her ability to surrender and rest in the palms of God's hand was truly admirable. After all the hardships she had endured. Shamu, in my eyes, was unshakable. Her faith was unwavering. I remembered what Guruji had said about faith.

"Faith brings stability, centeredness, calmness and love. Such strength one gets just by having faith."

Thirty minutes later, Shamu came out of the hospital consultation room with a relieved look on her face.

From Question to Quest

"The results are ALL CLEAR." She said with a sigh.

We were so relieved. A burden of panic had just been lifted from Shamu's face as we took the Matatu back to Shamu's house.

"Jesus has taken care of me today, and I have been waiting for two weeks with uncertainty not knowing what would happen." Shamu said, she looks so relieved.

The journey back to the island was filled with moments of silence, profound wisdom and many tears of relief.

"I pray for you Maaya." Shamu said.

"What are you praying for?" I asked in a subdued way.

"Maaya, I pray that you believe again in life. May you believe in the beauty of life and all the opportunities it brings you. Whatever is happening, it's happening for your highest good." Shamu said.

Chapter 10

"Shamu, how do you cultivate your faith when you have endured so many hardships? God seems to be continuously testing you!" I asked her curiously.

"Faith works that way my dear. There is no room for doubt. If the results were not as expected, that too would have been embraced. Faith tells me that no matter what lies ahead of me, God is already there. We must trust God's plan. Seeing life as a journey and surrendering to what will be is the only way forward. In surrender, we learn to do our best and then rely on the higher intelligence to take over." she said, holding my hand tightly and smiling.

My eyes gazed at the floor.

"Everything will be okay Maaya!" Shamu said.

After pausing, she softly spoke, "After all, we are all pearls on a string Maaya."

"What do you mean by that?" I asked.

Shamu said, "Each one of us is a special pearl in this universe, and there is something unseen that binds us all together, just like the string of a pearl necklace. Individually we are simply pearls but together we are connected by this creation of divinity."

A ball of fear swept me off guard as I started to doubt my journey again. I wanted to understand the bigger picture of what was going on but didn't know how to connect the dots together. That afternoon we waved Ali Baba and Shamu goodbye. I hugged Shamu tight.

"I will never forget you Shamu — you have taught me so much in the last few days and I am so grateful to have met you."

"Me too." She replied.

"Now remember what I said. Trust the universe and when you don't know what to do, simply sit and wait for the deepest ache to rise from within and pray. Wait for the answer. Surrender and let the answer reveal itself."

The next day Naomi and I got ready for our tandem skydive to raise funds for Tumaini's Home of Hope. My stomach coiled into a ball of nervous energy. The first question that raced through my mind is "WHAT IF I DIE?"

Chapter 10

My skydiving master, Claudius from Hamburg, Germany was a bald man in his mid-forties. He looked a little intimidating and I began to shrink into my own body, petrified.

"Read this over and over again for the next 10 minutes," he said, handing me a piece of paper. He instructed both Naomi and me to read it out aloud.

"I must not fear. Fear is the mind-killer. Fear is the little-death that brings total obliteration. I will face my fear. I will permit it to pass over me and through me. And when it has gone past I will turn the inner eye to see its path. Where the fear has gone there will be nothing. Only I will remain."

"Read it firmly. Get into the state. Feel the words and face the FEAR." Claudius repeated.

I gulped down gallons of water to cool me down. My palms felt sweaty and my stomach churned. A rush of adrenaline rocketed through my veins. I found it hard to keep centered. I was SHIT SCARED!

"You have to put your legs behind my butt and put your hands together on your chest. The body should be a banana shape." He said, in a German accent.

My legs felt like jelly. We stepped inside the miniature plane. Only six seats were to be seen. As the plane increased its distance from the ground, I became more and more petrified.

My heartbeat was racing even faster. The question about death raced through my mind again and again. We eventually reached 12000 feet, by which time I felt suffocated and felt I was seriously losing my mind. The sheer height, I couldn't grasp it! The altitude! I wanted to escape, but there was no turning back. The plane door suddenly slammed open and the sheer gust of the wind blew on my face.

I somersaulted three times and plummeted down towards the Earth. The sheer altitude…30 seconds into the sky-dive I was jolted by the opening of the parachute, and then all of a sudden I was gliding, flying like a bird. I noticed the scenery; Nyali Beach, the sea, turquoise in colour, the sun rays shimmering. Time halted for only a few milliseconds, but felt like a long passage of time.

Chapter 10

The rush of adrenalin gradually subsided as we landed and cheered everyone on. We took our jumpsuits off and celebrated.

I felt elated and fatigued simultaneously.

I survived…

Hooray…

I am alive!!

Naomi and I excitedly hugged each other tightly. I felt liberated. I had conquered my fear. Wow, what an accomplishment. What a day.

HOLY SHIT!

Another FEAR CONQUERED!!

WHAT AN ACCOMPLISHMENT!!!

Chapter 11

Connecting the Dots

"Again you can't connect the dots looking forward; you can only connect them looking backwards. So you have to trust that the dots will somehow — connect in your future. Trust in something — your gut, destiny, life, karma, whatever. This approach has never let me down and it has made all the difference in my life."

— *Steve Jobs*

Feeling free and more at peace with myself I opened the scroll from Baba and read;

"You are not here to play small. Tap into the power of your dreams and pursue them. The potential for greatness lies within all of us."

The next day Naomi and I were walking along Agha Khan Road absorbing the chaos of a Saturday afternoon in Mombasa, when a sudden parade of protesters came out of nowhere. Feeling a little jolted, we quickly snuck into the nearest place which coincidentally happened to be church. As we

Chapter 11

entered the church, our world transcended from the hustle and bustle of Mombasa to a blissful oracle of serenity.

It was surreal. Naomi and I were both immersed in an envelope of silence. A few people were seated at the front as we approached the seats of the beautiful church. I took a moment to admire the shimmering colours of the stained-glass windows. The musician was playing the organ and singing in a mystical voice. What was silence for my mind was music for my soul. I felt like my very essence was illuminated by the sacred chanting. What was this magnificence that captured us? I recollected in astonishment, smiling in reverence?

This was a sacred moment and I began to feel the warm heat flow through my body. I felt spiritually uplifted. Naomi and I looked at one other smiling. Neither of us spoke. Our hearts knew instinctively what we had experienced. We spent time absorbed in silence. Such presence... such bliss... such liberation. I remembered what Guruji taught us, 'The quieter you become the more you can hear.'

Later on that day, I excitedly skipped to the temple to tell Guruji about my journey. I wanted to tell him I had begun to feel whole again. But Guruji had left to go to Bangalore.

Paddy said, "His work had finished here."

I was a little dismayed as we had spent so much time together. How could he leave without saying goodbye?

I turned back from the temple and decided to take a walk on the beach to reflect on my journey. 'The ocean is infinite and so are we.' I thought. The sun was at its cusp, about to set, and looked like an electric ball of fire. As I was walking along, I noticed the grains of sand wash over my feet. I looked up at the sky and noticed three clouds shaped like angels with wings. I stood there staring in wonderment.

Was this a sign from the universe speaking to me? Guruji had spoken up about being taken care of and Shamu advised to look out for the signs and listen to the whispers of the universe. My heart skipped a beat or two, I felt giddy. Happy for no reason…joyful from within…I was tempted to ask someone on the beach if they saw what I saw, just to check I wasn't going delirious. But as I closed

Chapter 11

my eyes and took a deep breath I heard my inner voice talking to me.

'The universe is speaking to you… LISTEN.'

I took a few more deep breaths and observed the angels; the images became sharper. Just then Muffin, Naomi's furry friend, came running towards me, wagging his tail. As I welcomed him in my open arms, he gave me his paw and affectionately licked my face. Both Muffin and I sat on the beach and embraced the precious moment. Muffin looked into my eyes, stared at me, then looked up at the angels.

I knew he was trying to tell me something. I need not feel lonely… that all that I needed was right here in this moment. For the first time, I felt my Baba's presence right next to me, warming my heart. I felt so grateful for this journey. I returned to my hostel and opened the last scroll from Baba. The scroll titled 'The mysterious, make life a celebration.' Baba ended his gift of letters with this final piece of advice:

"Deep inside of you beyond your circumstances and situations lies the supreme self that is eternally at peace. Untouched and untethered. Nothing can touch you. Being a witness to ALL THAT IS, collecting the precious moments that matter is all that counts. Go deep within and remember that you are here for a bigger purpose. What is your purpose?"

Tears ran down my cheeks, a ball of gratitude in my heart inflated like a pink balloon, permeating through my body. I was recollecting all the blessings I had received on this miraculous journey. The seva day at Tumaini, meeting Guruji, attending the happiness course, learning the Sudarshan Kriya, understanding yoga as a form of spiritual balance and evolution, Kimji's message after seva day, experiencing silence, the church moment with Naomi, Paddy's coaching sessions, the evening with Shamu. The list was endless.

I came out to fulfil Baba's wishes, and in the end it was me who healed. My emotional pain about Raj had subsided. No longer did I have the intensity of hurt that consumed my body and mind. Instead I made a commitment to myself that I was going to show up differently. With kindness,

Chapter 11

empathy and cooperation, and embrace my divorce with a level of maturity.

I had met with a sense of freedom. I felt liberated. I could now see so clearly. I began to realise there was a higher intelligence at play. At that moment I began to reflect on what I had learnt about faith. Those that have faith believe in the miraculous. They believe and trust that whatever is happening in their lives is happening for their highest good and there is a reason behind it.

Guruji's wisdom echoed in my mind, 'The whole cosmos is inextricably woven together so everyone and everything is interconnected. When you are happy for no reason and you don't attach your happiness to anything or anyone. You become free.'

While walking back to the hostel, a feather landed on my toes. I grinned at the sheer synchronicities that were occurring one after the other. Mother Nature was cradling me in her arms and I could feel the presence of my Baba.

I connected to my heart and listened to my intuition. A voice spoke to me. 'Trust the cosmos.

From Question to Quest

Connect the dots Maaya. See life broadly. Listen to the whispers of your heart Maaya and let your heart guide you. That is where the peace is. Connect to this very truth. Everything is temporary. Anicca, Anicca, Anicca. This life is very brief, ephemeral. 60, 70, 80 years. You will be finished—everything will be gone. Who will know that you even existed? Wake up and see the impermanence life. Now wake up." I knew that voice was Guruji.

I arrived back at the hostel and started to get ready for my flight home. Naomi and Paddy came to see me off at the airport. While I was excited to be going home with a renewed feeling from this healing journey, I was sad that I was leaving behind these friends who had played such a significant role in my growth and healing.

"Paddy, you have truly empowered and inspired me to live my best life…THANK YOU!" I said as I gave him a tight hug.

"I have had a few light bulb moments because of the coaching sessions Paddy!"

Chapter 11

"Well they don't call me a catalyst for nothing. It's been my joy to be part of your journey—remember this is the start of a new life for you. Just be gentle with yourself, OKAY?"

I hugged Paddy again and nodded.

"Maaya, it's been amazing! His whole journey, and connecting with you…Of course our church moment was something very sacred." Naomi said.

"Absolutely, very precious." I said.

I opened my gratitude journal and started writing out all the positive blessings, cultivating this new habit. This new chapter was the start of something big. These moments were precious and my spirit was beaming with joy. I had found myself.

After the coaching sessions with Paddy, I made a conscious decision not to waste a single day wallowing about my own life's trials. I knew that how I shaped my life going forward was a tribute to my Baba and I was determined to keep his memory alive. I had learnt the powerful tools of yoga and Kriya to develop resilience.

From Question to Quest

Paddy's life coaching gave me a blueprint to cultivate my life which was now filled with a renewed sense of choice, passion and purpose. Nothing was going to stop me.

I felt blessed.

THE END

Chapter 11

From Question to Quest

"Dear Maaya, I never left. Baba."

Chapter 11

"We have stopped for a moment to encounter each other, to meet, to love, to share. This is a precious moment, but it is transient. It is a little parenthesis in eternity. If we share with caring, lightheartedness, and love, we will create abundance and joy for each other. And then this moment will have been worthwhile."

—Deepak Chopra.

From Question to Quest

Resources

Founded in 1981, by H.H. Sri Sri Ravi Shankar, the Art of Living Foundation is a non-profit educational and humanitarian organization that offers effective educational and self-development programs and tools that facilitate the elimination of stress and foster deep and profound inner peace, happiness and wellbeing.

These programs include breathing techniques, meditation, yoga, and practical wisdom. They have helped millions around the world to completely transform their lives by eliminating stress and achieving clarity in the mind and strength in the body.

In 2020, over 30 million people across the globe logged online to meditate daily with H.H Sri Sri Ravi Shankar during the Covid 19 pandemic, giving people a sense of strength, hope and peace during a time of uncertainty and turmoil.

Sri Sri's mission is to help individuals to find peace within oneself and to unite people in our society from all different cultures, religions and nationalities, reminding us that we have one goal;

Resources

to uplift human life everywhere. The Art of Living is present in 152 countries, reaching an estimated 300 million people worldwide, with a vision of individual and social stewardship in society.

For more information, please visit:

www.artofliving.org/uk-en

For research into yoga and meditation practices please visit the following sites:

https://scholar.harvard.edu/sara_lazar/home

https://www.ikyta.org/teachers/satbir

https://www.themindfulnessinitiative.org/

Printed in Great Britain
by Amazon

Foreword by Vishal Morjaria
Award Winning Author and International Speaker

Maaya Thacker was living proof that having it all wasn't enough. Married to the man of her dreams, Maaya was convinced that she had found her happily ever after. However, deep down a different story emerged as Maaya felt a void that just wouldn't go away. Then came judgement day. Maaya's father suddenly died; her marriage torpedoed into disaster leaving her stranded on the edge of an emotional abyss. Left broken and grief stricken, she set out on a quest in search for meaning where she discovered a magical treasure she never knew existed. Her life changed forever.

- A compelling story with nuggets of wisdom that will inspire you to tap into your personal power to become your best self.

- Practical wisdom on how to create meaning from the events that occur in your life, rekindling the faith to bring about personal transformation.

ABOUT THE AUTHOR

Krishna is an experienced CIPD qualified HR professional with a background in Occupational Psychology. She has spent the last 15 years in HR specializing in Learning & Development, Leadership and Coaching. Having worked at a large number of blue-chip organisations, Krishna's mission is to empower others to unleash their own potential, help people find their passion, purpose and live a life of abundance and fulfilment.

Learn more about Krishna
www.unshakableresilience.com

£20.00 $25.00 €22.92

ISBN 9781686079771